MW00487871

Vocabulary Booster

Book One

by
Dr. William Kottmeyer
and
Audrey Claus

PROPERTY OF THE
SCHOOL DEPARTMENT
TOWN OF CUMBERLAND
RHODE ISLAND

Phoenix Learning Resources
New York

Copyright © 1989 by Phoenix Learning Resources, Inc.
All Rights Reserved. No part of this publication may
be reproduced, stored in a retrieval system, or transmitted,
in any form or by any means, electronic, mechanical, recording,
photocopying, or otherwise, without the prior written
permission of the publisher. Printed in the United States
of America.

ISBN 0-7915-2800-6

4 5 6 7 8 9 0 99 98

Contents

Lesson 1
Vocabulary

1. **stare** _____ / stãr / verb
   synonyms: look, gaze
   The children <u>stared</u> at the stranger.
   homonym: stair
   We went up the <u>stairs</u> to the attic.

---

2. **leap** _____ / lēp / verb
   synonyms: jump, spring
   The child <u>leaped</u> for joy.
   The man <u>leaped</u> for his car.

---

3. **trot** _____ / trot / verb
   synonym: jog
   Horses <u>trot</u>.
   The little boy <u>trotted</u> home happily.

---

4. **seize** _____ /sēz / verb
   synonym: grab
   The fox <u>seized</u> a hen and ran off with it.
   noun: seizure

---

5. **pant** _____ / pant / verb
   synonyms: breathe (hard), gasp
   Runners pant after a race.
   Dogs pant in summer.

6. **attempt** _____ / ə tempt′ / noun, verb
   synonym: try
   He made an attempt to catch the ball. (noun)
   He attempted to catch it. (verb)

7. **gleam** _____ /glēm / noun, verb
   synonyms: shine, sparkle
   Candles make a soft gleam. (noun)
   Candles gleamed on the table. (verb)

8. **famish** _____ / fam′ ish / verb
   synonym: starve
   Cattle may famish in a snow storm.
   adjective: famished

9. **exhaust** _____ / ig zôst′ / noun, verb
   Hard work exhausts us. (verb)
   Exhaust from a car is poisonous. (noun)
   noun: exhaustion
   adjectives: exhausted, exhaustive

10. **splendid** _____ / splen′ did / adjective
    synonyms: grand, glorious, brilliant
    The queen wore a splendid gown.
    noun: splendor

Lesson 1.
The Fox and the Grapes

Fox was hungry. He patted his empty stomach with his paw.

"I am <u>famished</u>," he said. "I will have to find food. There must be something good to eat out there in the woods."

Off <u>trotted</u> the fox. Soon he saw some ripe blue grapes hanging on a vine high above his head. Fox's eyes <u>gleamed</u>. He smacked his lips.

"I am in luck!" he cried. "What <u>splendid</u> grapes!"

He <u>trotted</u> back a few steps, broke into a run, and <u>leaped</u> high into the air. He missed the grapes by at least a foot. He <u>trotted</u> back again for a second <u>attempt</u>. He ran. He <u>leaped</u> once more. Again he missed the grapes by nine or ten inches.

Fox <u>attempted</u> again and again to <u>seize</u> the grapes in his teeth. Again and again his <u>leap</u> fell a few inches short of the grapes.

At last he was <u>exhausted</u>. <u>Panting</u>, he sat down in the shade. He <u>stared</u> at the grapes. At last he got up and <u>trotted</u> off into the woods.

"Shucks!" he said. "Those grapes are sour! Who wants to eat sour grapes?"

Lesson 2
Vocabulary

1. **greed** _____ / grēd / noun
   The miser had <u>greed</u> for gold.
   adjective: greedy
   adverb: greedily

2. **choice** _____ / chois / noun, adjective
   Mary's <u>choice</u> was a blue silk dress. (noun)
   <u>Choice</u> fruit is on sale at the market. (adjective)

3. **feast** _____ / fēst / noun, verb
   The Pilgrims had a Thanksgiving <u>feast</u>. (noun)
   They <u>feasted</u> on turkey, corn, and squash. (verb)

4. **stream** _____ / strēm / noun, verb
   We waded across the <u>stream</u>. (noun)
   Fans <u>streamed</u> out of the ball park. (verb)
   related words: streamer, streamline

5. **pause** _____ / pôz / noun, verb
After a short pause, we went on our way. (noun)
The pitcher paused before throwing the ball. (verb)
homonym: paws
The kitten's paws have sharp claws.

6. **glance** _____ / glans / noun, verb
The pitcher gave the runner a quick glance. (noun)
The pitcher glanced at the runner. (verb)

7. **reflection** _____ / ri flek′ shən / noun
synonym: image
You see your reflection in a mirror.
verb: reflect
related noun: reflector

8. **glare** _____ / glãr / noun, verb
The glare of the headlights almost blinded the driver. (noun)
The batter glared at the umpire. (verb)
adjective: glaring

9. **mutter** _____ / mut′ ər / verb
synonyms: grumble, complain
The driver muttered to himself when his car stalled.

10. **plunge** _____ / plunj / noun, verb
synonym: dive
A plunge in the swimming pool is fun. (noun)
The lifeguard plunged into the water to save the drowning child. (verb)

Lesson 2.
The Greedy Dog

Once upon a time a greedy dog saw a choice piece of meat hanging on a neighbor's porch. His eyes gleamed with greed.

"What a splendid feast I could have if I succeed in stealing that meat. I am famished!" he cried.

The dog leaped high, seized the meat, and trotted off for home. The dog had to cross a bridge over a swift stream of water on his way home. As he was trotting across the bridge, he paused to glance downward. Of course he saw his reflection staring up at him. The dog glared back.

"His piece of meat is as fine as mine," he muttered. "If I could have his, too, I could have a splendid feast!"

Overcome by his greed, the dog plunged into the stream to seize the other dog's meat.

Of course, the dog's attempt resulted only in the loss of his own meat. Exhausted and half drowned, he crawled panting to shore, a sadder and wiser dog.

Lesson 3
Vocabulary

1. **clutch** _____ / kluch / noun, verb
   synonyms: grasp, grip, hold
   The child had a tight <u>clutch</u> on my hand. (noun)
   She <u>clutched</u> my hand. (verb)

---

2. **devise** _____ / di vīz' / verb
   synonyms: invent, plan
   We must <u>devise</u> a way to earn some money.

---

3. **shrewd** _____ / shrüd / adjective
   synonym: clever
   Mr. Smith is a <u>shrewd</u> businessman.
   noun: shrewdness
   adverb: shrewdly

---

4. **scheme** _____ / skēm / noun, verb
   synonyms: plan, plot
   There is a <u>scheme</u> for getting salt from the sea. (noun)
   The men <u>schemed</u> to steal the jewels. (verb)
   adjective: scheming

---

5. **vain** _____ / vān / adjective
   synonym: conceited
   Vain people often boast.
   homonyms: vein, vane
   Veins carry blood to the heart.
   We put a weather vane on the barn.
   noun: vanity

6. **devour** _____ / di vour′ / verb
   synonym: eat (greedily)
   Dogs devour meat.

7. **delight** _____ / di līt′ / noun, verb
   synonyms: joy, pleasure (noun); please (verb)
   It's a delight to hear him sing. (noun)
   His singing delighted everyone. (verb)
   adjective: delightful

8. **delicate** _____ / del′ ə kit / adjective
   synonyms: weak, flimsy
   A spider's web is delicate.
   noun: delicacy

9. **vocal** _____ / vō′ kəl / adjective
   The choir gave a program of vocal music.

10. **talent** _____ / tal′ ənt / noun
    synonyms: ability, gift
    She has talent in art.
    adjective: talented

Lesson 3.
The Fox and
the Vain Crow

As usual, Fox was hungry. <u>Exhausted</u> from <u>trotting</u> through the woods all morning, he <u>paused</u> at a cool <u>stream</u> for a drink. Still <u>panting</u> hard, he <u>glanced</u> upward. There on a limb he saw a crow <u>glaring</u> down at him. In her beak she <u>clutched</u> a <u>choice</u> piece of cheese. Fox's eyes <u>gleamed</u>.

"What a <u>splendid</u> <u>feast</u> that cheese would make," <u>muttered</u> the <u>famished</u> fox. "I must <u>attempt</u> to <u>devise</u> a <u>scheme</u> to get it before that <u>vain</u> old bird <u>devours</u> it herself."

"Is that you, Crow?" he cried, <u>staring</u> upward. "The bird with the most <u>delicate</u> singing voice in the whole world? Please, give us one of your charming tunes, I beg you! You do have such great <u>vocal</u> <u>talent</u> my dear!"

<u>Delighted</u> with the <u>shrewd</u> fox's praise, the <u>vain</u> old crow opened her beak to sing. As she let out the hoarse croak that crows make, the cheese <u>plunged</u> to the ground. Fox <u>leaped</u> up, <u>seized</u> it in his <u>greedy</u> jaws, and <u>trotted</u> off into the woods with a sly grin on his face.

Lesson 4
Vocabulary

1. **frequently** _____ / frē kwənt′ lē / adverb
   synonym: often
   It rains <u>frequently</u> in spring.
   adjective: frequent

---

2. **annoy** _____ / ə noi′ / verb
   synonyms: disturb, bother, vex
   Barking dogs often <u>annoy</u> people.
   noun: annoyance
   adjective: annoying

---

3. **generous** _____ / jen′ ər əs / adjective
   That man is <u>generous</u> with his money.
   I ate a <u>generous</u> serving of salad.
   noun: generosity

---

4. **accept** _____ / ak sept′ / verb
   Everyone has <u>accepted</u> our invitation.
   noun: acceptance
   adjective: acceptable

---

5. **startle** _____ / stär′ təl / verb
   synonyms: frighten, shock
   Loud noises <u>startle</u> babies.
   adjective: startling

6. **guest** _____ / gest / noun
   synonym: visitor
   We had six <u>guests</u> for dinner.

7. **delicious** _____ / di lish′ əs / adjective
   We ate a <u>delicious</u> picnic lunch.

8. **suspect** _____ / sə spekt′ / verb
   _____ / sus′ pekt / noun, adjective
   I <u>suspect</u> that man stole my ring. (verb)
   He is a <u>suspect</u> in the crime. (noun)
   His actions are <u>suspect</u>. (adjective)
   related noun: suspicion

9. **host** _____ / hōst / noun
   Bob was the <u>host</u> of a party at his house.
   A <u>host</u> of stars are shining.
   related noun: hostess

10. **murmur** _____ / mer′ mər / noun, verb
    synonyms: whisper, mumble
    We heard the <u>murmur</u> of voices. (noun)
    She <u>murmured</u> that she was sleepy. (verb)

Lesson 4.
The Fox
and the Stork

Fox was a shrewd fellow, but he frequently took delight in playing mean tricks on his friends. He once devised a sly scheme to annoy his friend Stork.

"Stork," he said, "do come over to my place this evening for dinner. We'll have a splendid feast. I have quite a talent for cooking, you know."

"That's very generous of you, Fox," said Stork. "I'll be delighted to accept your invitation."

When Stork sat down to eat at Fox's table, he was startled to see a flat dish set before him.

"Have some of this choice soup, Stork," he said to his guest. "It's delicious."

He poured a stream of steaming hot soup into the two flat dishes. Stork did not even attempt to eat his soup through his long, thin bill. Fox plunged right in and devoured his soup greedily. He simply lapped it up from the flat dish. Fox paused and glanced at his guest's full dish.

"I was famished," he said. "I'm sorry you don't care for the soup, Stork." He patted his belly and grinned.

A month later Stork invited Fox to dinner. Fox, not suspecting a trick, accepted. Fox was surprised when Stork set two vases with long, thin necks on the table. As the host, Stork poured a stream of hot soup into the vases.

"Help yourself, Fox," he said. "This choice soup has a fine, delicate taste."

Stork pushed his long, thin bill easily into his vase and devoured his soup. Of course, Fox could not get at his soup at all. He licked his vase in vain.

"Delicious!" murmured Stork. "Sorry you don't care for the soup, Fox." He patted his belly with his wing and grinned.

Fox trotted home, muttering about hosts who delighted in annoying their guests.

Lesson 5
Vocabulary

1. **toil** _____ / toil / noun, verb
   synonyms: work, labor
   Chopping wood is <u>toil</u>. (noun)
   The farmer <u>toiled</u> all day in his field. (verb)

_____

2. **merry** _____ / mer′ ē / adjective
   synonyms: joyous, happy
   We had a <u>merry</u> time at the party.
   nouns: merriment, merrymaker, merrymaking, merry-go-round
   adverb: merrily

_____

3. **colony** _____ / kol′ o nē / noun
   Virginia was one of thirteen original <u>colonies</u>.
   verb: colonize
   adjective: colonial / kə lō′ nē əl /
   related noun: colonist

_____

4. **retort** _____ / ri tôrt′ / noun, verb
   synonyms: reply, answer, comeback
   "It's none of your business," he <u>retorted</u>. (verb)
   He gave a sassy <u>retort</u>. (verb)

_____

5. **regret** _____ / ri gret' / noun, verb
   I regret missing the meeting. (verb)
   I have regrets about what I did wrong. (noun)
   adjectives: regretful, regrettable

6. **survive** _____ / sər vīv' / verb
   synonym: live
   Some plants can't survive in winter.
   nouns: survivor, survival

7. **severe** _____ / sə vir' / adjective
   synonyms: harsh, stern, bad
   A severe storm damaged the trees.
   He deserves severe punishment for the crime.
   noun: severity

8. **feeble** _____ / fē' bəl / adjective
   synonym: weak
   antonym: strong
   Great grandmother is quite feeble now, but once she was a strong woman.

9. **perish** _____ / per' ish / verb
   synonym: die
   antonyms: live, survive
   Two sailors perished in the shipwreck, but a hundred others survived.

10. **gasp** _____ / gasp / noun, verb
    He gave a gasp of surprise. (noun)
    He gasped when he saw his new bike. (verb)
    "Help!" gasped the drowning man. (verb)

Lesson 5.
The Grasshopper and the Ants

"Ant," said the Grasshopper, "I don't mean to <u>annoy</u> you, but why must you <u>toil</u> the whole day long? Come play with me. I have such a <u>delightful</u> time singing <u>merry</u> songs. I <u>leap</u> from plant to plant <u>devouring</u> <u>delicious</u> green leaves."

Ant did not even <u>pause</u> to <u>glance</u> at Grasshopper.

"Our ant <u>colony</u> is preparing for winter," <u>retorted</u> Ant. "We have none of your <u>vocal</u> <u>talent</u> for singing <u>merry</u> tunes. The cold winds will blow more <u>frequently</u>. The snow will fall. You will live to <u>regret</u> your foolish words. The streams will freeze. You will never <u>survive</u> a <u>severe</u> winter!"

Indeed, the summer was soon over. The cold winds did blow more <u>frequently</u>, and the snow fell in great drifts. Grasshopper attempted in <u>vain</u> to find food. At last he fell, <u>exhausted</u> and <u>panting</u> at the door of the anthill.

"Maybe my friends, the ants, will be <u>generous</u> and take me in," he <u>muttered</u>. "Help!" he cried in a <u>feeble</u> voice. "I am <u>famished</u>!"

But the <u>shrewd</u> ants were not willing to play <u>hosts</u> to hungry <u>guests</u>. Soon Grasshopper <u>clutched</u> his throat, <u>gasped</u>, and <u>perished</u>.

Lesson 6
Vocabulary

1. **reduce** _____ / ri dūs' / or / ri dus' / verb
   synonyms: decrease, lessen, lower
   antonyms: increase, raise
   Food prices have been <u>reduced</u>, but clothing prices have been raised.
   noun: reduction

___

2. **poverty** _____ / pov' ər tē / noun
   antonym: wealth
   The rich man lost his wealth and now lives in <u>poverty</u>.
   adjective: poverty-stricken

___

3. **wealth** _____ / welth / noun
   synonym: riches
   antonym: poverty
   adjective: wealthy
   Her <u>wealth</u>, five million dollars, came from the lottery.

___

4. **amazement** _____ / ə māz' mənt / noun
   synonyms: surprise, wonder
   The moon landing filled us with <u>amazement</u>.
   verb: amaze
   adjective: amazing

___

5. **propose** _____ / prə pōz' / verb
   synonym: suggest
   I <u>propose</u> that we go skating.
   nouns: proposal, proposition

___

6. **cease** _____ / sēs / verb
   synonym: stop
   The noise must <u>cease</u>!
   adjective: ceaseless
   adverb: ceaselessly

7. **folly** _____ / fol' ē / noun
   synonym: foolishness
   antonym: wisdom
   Wasting time is <u>folly</u>, but using it well shows wisdom.

8. **resolve** _____ / ri zolv' / noun, verb
   verb synonym: decide
   noun synonym: determination
   Pat <u>resolved</u> to study more. (verb)
   His <u>resolve</u> is to work harder. (noun)
   related noun: resolution
   adjective: resolute

9. **fortune** _____ / fôr' chən / noun
   synonyms: wealth, luck
   antonym: misfortune
   She has a <u>fortune</u> in the bank.
   Rain can be good <u>fortune</u> for farmers and <u>misfortune</u> for picnickers.
   adjective: fortunate

10. **dismay** _____ / dis mā' / noun, verb
    He was <u>dismayed</u> by the loss of his job. (verb)
    Loss of a job causes great <u>dismay</u>. (noun)

Lesson 6.
The Goose and the Golden Eggs

After years of hard <u>toil</u>, an old man and his wife were <u>reduced</u> to <u>severe</u> <u>poverty</u>. All they had left of their <u>wealth</u> was a goose. This goose laid one egg every morning, making it possible for the <u>feeble</u> old pair to <u>survive</u>.

One morning the old man <u>trotted</u> down to the barn to get the egg, as usual. He was <u>startled</u> when a <u>gleam</u> of light from the nest struck his eye. The old man <u>stared</u>, then <u>gasped</u> in <u>amazement</u>. The goose had laid a golden egg! He <u>seized</u> the egg and ran to show it to his wife. The old lady <u>clutched</u> the egg in her hands as tears of joy <u>streamed</u> down her cheeks.

The goose laid a golden egg every day, and the old couple soon became <u>wealthy</u>. As he became richer, the old man became <u>greedier</u> and <u>greedier</u>.

"I <u>suspect</u> that our goose is all gold inside," he said to his wife. "Think of all the money we could get for her if I killed her. I <u>propose</u> that we do so."

"What a silly <u>scheme</u>!" she <u>retorted</u> in <u>dismay</u>. "Don't you dare kill the goose that lays our <u>splendid</u> golden eggs. You'll never <u>cease</u> to <u>regret</u> such <u>folly</u>."

But the <u>greedy</u> old man was <u>resolved</u> to kill the goose. <u>Seizing</u> the goose by the neck, he <u>plunged</u> his knife into the bird's chest. Of course he found no gold. The old couple soon spent their <u>fortune</u> and were poor as ever.

Lesson 7
Vocabulary

1. **discuss** _____ / dis kus' / verb
We have much to <u>discuss</u> at the meeting.
noun: discussion

---

2. **constant** _____ / kon' stənt / adjective
synonyms: unchanging, faithful, loyal, ceaseless, continual
antonyms: changing, unfaithful, disloyal
We had <u>constant</u> rain today.
Mike has been a <u>constant</u> friend who has never been disloyal.
noun: constancy
adverb: constantly

---

3. **enable** _____ / en ā' bəl / verb
Wind <u>enables</u> sailboats to move.

---

4. **pounce** _____ / pouns / noun, verb
The cat <u>pounced</u> on the mouse. (verb)
The cat made a <u>pounce</u> on the mouse. (noun)

---

5. **presence** _____ / prez' əns / noun
   antonym: absence
   Jim has had too many absences.
   We need his presence at the meeting.

6. **scamper** _____ / skam' pər / noun, verb
   Mice scamper when they see a cat. (verb)
   I let our dog outside for a scamper. (noun)

7. **moment** _____ / mō' mənt / noun
   synonyms: instant, importance
   I'll be ready in a moment.
   Elections are matters of great moment.
   adjectives: momentary, momentous

8. **applause** _____ / ə plôz' / noun
   synonyms: praise, approval
   The actor was pleased by the applause of the audience.
   verb: applaud

9. **modest** _____ / mod' ist / adjective
   synonyms: humble, bashful, shy
   antonyms: bold, vain, boastful
   Sue is modest about her talent and never vain or boastful.
   noun: modesty

10. **volunteer** _____ / vol ən tir' / noun, verb
    I volunteer to help plan the party. (verb)
    Ray is a volunteer in the library. (noun)
    adjective: voluntary
    adverb: voluntarily

Lesson 7.
Belling the Cat

A colony of mice was meeting to discuss their most severe problem—the cat!

"I am dismayed to have to live in constant fear of that greedy monster!" cried one mouse.

"Cat is shrewd," said another mouse. "Her soft paws frequently enable her to creep up on us without warning. Then she pounces on our friends and devours them. Oh, dear, I suspect we must all perish!"

"Surely we have enough talent here to devise some kind of a scheme to warn us of her presence," murmured a feeble old mouse.

A young mouse rose to speak.

"The problem is simple," he said. "I propose that we hang a bell around Cat's neck. Then, when she moves, the bell will ring and warn us. We can all scamper to safety."

There was a moment of silence. After the pause the delighted mice broke into loud applause. All clapped their paws and joined in giving the startled young mouse three ringing cheers. The young mouse bowed his head and stared modestly at the floor.

After the applause had died down, an old gray mouse spoke up.

"Who's going to bell the cat?" he asked.

There was a long silence. Nobody volunteered. The young mouse did not volunteer, either.

Lesson 8
Vocabulary

1. **inspect** _____ / in spekt' / v.
   synonym: examine
   Police <u>inspected</u> the room for clues.
   nouns: inspection, inspector

---

2. **curious** _____ / kūr' ē əs / adj.
   synonyms: inquisitive, nosey, unusual
   People are <u>curious</u> about Mars.
   Anteaters are <u>curious</u> looking animals.
   noun: curiosity

---

3. **plump** _____ / plump / n., v., adj.
   synonyms: chubby, fat (adj.)
   antonyms: scrawny, skinny, thin (adj.)
   That <u>plump</u> baby has a skinny brother. (adj.)
   Apples <u>plumped</u> from the tree. (v.)
   Each apple hit the ground with a <u>plump</u>. (n.)

---

4. **sleek** _____ / slēk / v., adj.
   synonyms: smooth, glossy (adj.)
   antonyms: rough, shaggy (adj.)
   Boxer dogs have <u>sleek</u> coats, but sheep dogs have shaggy fur. (adj.)
   The boy <u>sleeked</u> his hair with hair oil. (v.)

---

5. **envy** _____ / en′ vē / n., v.
   synonym: jealousy (n.)
   Tom envied Bill's pony. (v.)
   He was filled with envy for the pony. (n.)
   adjective: envious

6. **secure** _____ / sə kūr′ / v., adj.
   I feel secure when the door is locked. (adj.)
   I secured the boat to the dock. (v.)
   Have you secured tickets for the show? (v.)
   noun: security

7. **request** _____ / ri kwest′ / n., v.
   synonym: ask (v.)
   I requested her to wait for me. (v.)
   My request was granted. (n.)

8. **spied** _____ / spīd / v.
   The hunters spied a deer in the woods.
   verb forms: spy, spied, spying
   noun: spy

9. **roam** _____ / rōm / v.
   synonym: wander
   We roamed through the woods.

10. **prefer** _____ / pri fer′ / v.
    I prefer apples to pears.
    verb forms: prefer, preferred, preferring
    noun: preference
    adjective: preferable
    adverb: preferably

Lesson 8.
The House Dog and the Wolf

One bright moonlit night a wolf met a house dog from a nearby farm. They <u>paused</u> to <u>inspect</u> each other <u>curiously</u>. The wolf <u>stared</u> at the dog as they <u>trotted</u> along.

"You look so <u>plump</u> and <u>sleek</u>," said the wolf. "I <u>suspect</u> you get plenty to eat, don't you?"

"Indeed, I do. They feed me <u>generously</u>. I <u>constantly</u> feast on <u>delicious</u> food."

"I <u>envy</u> you, Dog," cried the wolf bitterly. "I am <u>frequently</u> <u>famished</u> for days during <u>severe</u> winters. I barely <u>survive</u>. Could you <u>secure</u> me a place like yours as a watch dog?"

"I'm sure I can fix it," said the dog. "I'll be glad to <u>propose</u> your <u>request</u> to the farmer. Let's <u>trot</u> down to the farm and <u>discuss</u> it with the master."

As they <u>trotted</u> along, Wolf <u>spied</u> a bare place on the dog's neck. He asked him about it.

"Oh, my collar is <u>frequently</u> too tight and it rubs on my fur."

"Collar?"

"Yes. The collar to which my chain is fastened."

"Chain? Aren't you free to <u>roam</u> all day?"

"Oh, no. The farmer ties me up all day. I'm allowed to run free only at night to guard the place. I sleep all day. That <u>enables</u> me to be more <u>alert</u> at night. Say, Wolf, where are you going? I thought you <u>volunteered</u> to—"

"Good-bye, my friend. You may keep that splendid food. I <u>prefer</u> my freedom to your free food."

Lesson 9
Vocabulary

1. **village** _____ / vil′ ij / n.
   synonym: town
   Everyone in the <u>village</u> knows Dad.
   related noun: villager

---

2. **balance** _____ / bal′ əns / n., v.
   The seal <u>balanced</u> a ball on its nose. (v.)
   These two weights <u>balance</u>. (v.)
   I lost my <u>balance</u> and fell. (n.)
   I'll pay $10.00 now and the balance later. (n.)

---

3. **future** _____ / fu′ chər / n.
   In the <u>future</u>, don't borrow my pen.

---

4. **purchase** _____ / per′ chəs / n., v.
   synonym: buy (v.)
   antonym: sell (v.)
   I'll sell my wagon and <u>purchase</u> a bike. (v.)
   noun: purchaser

---

5. **noble** _____ / nō′ bəl / adj.
   synonyms: fine, good, excellent, splendid
   Knights did many <u>noble</u> deeds.
   Niagara Falls is a <u>noble</u> sight.
   nouns: noble, nobility

6. **seek** _____ / sēk / v.
   synonym: search (for)
   Most people <u>seek</u> happiness.
   verb forms: seek, sought, have sought

7. **toss** _____ / tôs / n., v.
   synonyms: throw, fling
   I <u>tossed</u> the dog a bone. (v.)
   The sick man <u>tossed</u> in his bed. (v.)
   She answered with a <u>toss</u> of her head. (n.)

8. **sneer** _____ / snir / n., v.
   Cinderella's sister <u>sneered</u> at her. (v.)
   The king gave the beggar a <u>sneer</u>. (n.)

9. **desperate** _____ / des′ pər it / adj.
   That dog is in <u>desperate</u> need of food.
   noun: desperation
   adverb: desperately

10. **wail** _____ / wāl / n., v.
    synonym: cry
    The child <u>wailed</u> with pain. (v.)
    We heard the <u>wail</u> of the wind. (n.)

Lesson 9.
The Foolish Milkmaid

A <u>vain</u> young milkmaid was on her way to the <u>village</u> to sell her pail of milk. As she <u>balanced</u> the pail on her head, she began to dream of the <u>future</u>.

"With the milk money I shall <u>purchase</u> some choice, plump hens," she <u>murmured</u>." The hens will lay lots of eggs. I'll sell the eggs for a small <u>fortune</u>. The egg money will <u>enable</u> me to buy a <u>splendid</u> new dress of silk. How the girls will <u>envy</u> me! <u>Charmed</u> by my <u>presence</u>, the <u>wealthy</u> young men will <u>stare</u> at me and <u>propose</u> to me. I <u>prefer</u> to wait, though, until a <u>noble</u> prince <u>seeks</u> my hand. I'll <u>sneer</u> at the young men and <u>toss</u> my head back like this—"

The foolish milkmaid <u>gasped</u> in <u>dismay</u> as she <u>muttered</u> these last words. The pail slipped from her <u>desperate</u> <u>clutch</u> and <u>plunged</u> to the ground.

"Oh, dear!" she <u>wailed</u>. "I must learn not to count my chickens before they hatch!"

Lesson 10
Vocabulary

1. **trudge** _____ / truj / n., v.
   synonyms: walk, plod
   The campers <u>trudged</u> up the hill. (v.)
   The <u>trudge</u> up the hill took an hour. (n.)

_____

2. **beast** _____ / bēst / n.
   A <u>beast</u> is a four-legged animal.
   adjective: beastly

_____

3. **hoist** _____ / hoist / n., v.
   synonyms: raise, lift, boost (v.), boost (n.)
   Sailors <u>hoist</u> sails. (v.)
   Dad gave Jimmy a <u>hoist</u> to his shoulders. (n.)

_____

4. **furious** _____ / fūr′ ē əs / adj.
   synonyms: angry, enraged, fierce
   Mom is <u>furious</u> about the broken lamp.
   A <u>furious</u> wind blew down the tree.
   noun: fury
   adverb: furiously

_____

5. **compel** _____ / kəm pel′ / v.
   synonym: force
   Rain <u>compelled</u> us to stay indoors.
   verb forms: compelled, compelling

6. **dismount** _____ / dis mount′ / v.
   antonym: mount
   Mary <u>mounted</u> her horse, rode two miles, and then <u>dismounted</u>.

7. **clamber** _____ / klam′ bər / v.
   synonyms: scramble, climb
   We <u>clambered</u> up the steep hill.

8. **indignant** _____ / in dig′ nənt / adj.
   I'm <u>indignant</u> when I see a helpless animal being mistreated.
   noun: indignation
   adverb: indignantly

9. **struggle** _____ / strug′ əl / n., v.
   synonyms: try, fight
   We <u>struggled</u> to lift the heavy box. (v.)
   The armies <u>struggled</u> fiercely. (v.)
   It was a <u>struggle</u> to lift the box. (n.)
   The colonists won their <u>struggle</u> for independence from England. (n.)
   adjective: struggling

10. **brute** _____ / brüt / n.
    An ox is a strong <u>brute</u>.
    noun: brutality
    adjective: brutal

Lesson 10.
The Farmer, the Son, and the Donkey

A farmer and his son were driving their donkey to the village to sell him. On the road they met some girls.

"Look!" cried one. "Those fools trudge along on foot when they could be riding that sleek, plump beast! What folly!"

The farmer hoisted his son on the donkey's back and went on. Soon they met some old men.

"Look!" cried an old man furiously." That lazy boy rides while his feeble old father is compelled to walk! Shame!

The startled farmer told his son to dismount and he himself clambered on the donkey's back. They went on. Soon they met some women and children.

"Look!" cried a young woman indignantly, "that great brute of a man rides and compels his poor exhausted little son to walk!"

Seeking again to please, the farmer requested his son to ride the donkey behind him. As they came to a swift stream near the village, they spied a housewife glaring at them.

Look!" she sneered. "Those lazy brutes make a poor little donkey carry them! They ought to be carrying the donkey!"

The farmer and his son dismounted, tied the donkey's feet together, and with a pole on their shoulders, carried the donkey over the bridge. The poor frightened beast, struggling desperately to get free, lost his balance. A moment later he slipped off the pole, plunged into the stream, and perished.

Lesson 11
Mastery Test

The Vocabulary Booster lesson for today is your Mastery Test for Lessons 1–10.

☐ Prepare for the Mastery Test by reviewing your notebook pages for Lessons 1–10.

☐ Your teacher will distribute the test. Underline the word or phrase that gives the best definition of the test word. The first one is done for you.

EXAMPLE:

1. **severe** a) harsh b) broken c) windy d) very tired

☐ Review the test with your teacher and class.

☐ Record your Mastery Test score on the Mastery Test Progress Chart at the back of the book.

Lesson 12
Vocabulary

1. **observe** _____ / əb zerv' / v.
   synonyms: watch, see, remark, celebrate, obey
   Have you ever <u>observed</u> ants at work?
   Please <u>observe</u> the spelling of this word.
   "This book is good," Pat <u>observed</u>.
   We <u>observe</u> Labor Day in September.
   Drivers must <u>observe</u> traffic laws.
   nouns: observation, observatory, observer
   adjective: observative, observant

---

2. **ancient** _____ / ān' shənt / adj.
   The pyramids of Egypt are <u>ancient</u>.
   noun: ancients

---

3. **common** _____ / kom' ən / adj.
   synonyms: familiar, public, ordinary
   antonym: uncommon
   Rain is <u>common</u> in Japan and uncommon is desert lands.
   Public parks are the <u>common</u> property of all citizens.
   In the U.S.A. all citizens are "<u>common</u> people."
   adverb: commonly

---

4. **knowledge** _____ / nol' ij / n.
   What you know is your <u>knowledge</u>.

---

5. **shrill** _____ / shril / adj.
A whistle has a shrill sound.

6. **inspire** _____ / in spīr' / v.
synonym: influence
The coach inspired us to play fair.
noun: inspiration
adjective: inspiring

7. **terror** _____ / ter' ər / n.
synonym: fear
Thunder fills my puppy with terror.
verb: terrorize
adjective: terrified

8. **prompt** _____ / prompt / v., adj.
synonym: punctual
John is prompt. He is on time. (adj.)
My curiosity prompted me to peek. (v.)
adverb: promptly

9. **pursuit** _____ / pər süt' / n.
synonyms: chase, interest
The dog is in pursuit of the cat.
Mike's pursuit is science.
verb: pursue

10. **bellow** _____ / bel' ō / n., v.
synonyms: roar, shout, yell
The sergeant bellowed orders. (v.)
His bellow sounded angry. (n.)

Lesson 12.
The Brave Donkey

A donkey and a rooster lived together on an African farm. One day a lion, the <u>noble</u> king of <u>beasts</u>, <u>wandered</u> by. <u>Observing</u> that the donkey was <u>plump</u> and <u>sleek</u>, the lion <u>resolved</u> to <u>pounce</u> upon him and have a <u>feast</u> in the near <u>future</u>.

In those <u>ancient</u> times, it was <u>common</u> <u>knowledge</u> that, <u>curiously</u>, nothing <u>annoyed</u> lions more that the <u>shrill</u> crowing of roosters. <u>Spying</u> the lion about to <u>leap</u> upon the donkey, the rooster crowed with all his might. The <u>startled</u> lion, who <u>inspired</u> <u>terror</u> among the other <u>beasts</u>, turned tail and <u>trotted</u> off.

The <u>astonished</u> donkey, <u>delighted</u> to see the proud lion's <u>dismay</u>, <u>promptly</u> set out in <u>furious</u> <u>pursuit</u>.

"Come back and fight, <u>brutal</u> coward!" he <u>bellowed</u>. "Are you afraid of me?"

He had <u>pursued</u> the <u>greedy</u> lion only a short distance when the lion turned, <u>seized</u> him in his claws, and <u>promptly</u> <u>devoured</u> him.

Lesson 13
Vocabulary

1. **ability** _____ / ə bil′ ə tē / n.
   synonyms: power, talent
   Birds have the ability to fly.
   Sue has ability in art.
   adjective: able

_____

2. **solve** _____ / solv / v.
   Can you solve this riddle?
   noun: solution
   adjective: solvable

_____

3. **drought** _____ / drout / n.
   drouth _____ / drouth / n.
   A drought is a long dry spell.

_____

4. **effort** _____ / ef′ ərt / n.
   She made an effort to be on time.
   It takes effort to run uphill.
   adjective: effortless

_____

5. **vicinity** _____ / və sin′ ə tē / n.
   synonym: neighborhood
   I live in the vicinity of the school.

6. **swoop** _____ / swüp / v.
   Crows swooped down on the field.
   Pirates swooped down on the village.
   Mother swooped the baby into her arms.

7. **peer** _____ / pir / v.
   synonyms: stare, gaze, peep
   I peered at the address on the postcard.
   The sun peered from the clouds.
   homograph: peer (an equal)
   homonym: pier (platform in the water)

8. **gradually** _____ / graj′ ü lē / adv.
   We gradually grow taller.

9. **proceed** _____ / prə sēd′ / v.
   The cars proceeded down the street.
   He proceeded to unlock the door.
   noun: procedure

10. **quench** _____ / kwench / v.
    synonyms: stop, end
    We quench our thirst by drinking water.
    Always quench a campfire before leaving it.

Lesson 13.
The Crow and the Pitcher

It is <u>common</u> <u>knowledge</u> that crows <u>frequently</u> show great <u>ability</u> to <u>solve</u> problems. Once upon a time, an old crow was caught in a <u>severe</u> <u>drought</u>. Desperately she <u>sought</u> (seek) water, but her <u>constant</u> <u>efforts</u> were in <u>vain</u>. The <u>streams</u> had dried up, and there were no ponds in the <u>vicinity</u>.

At last the crow <u>spied</u> a water pitcher standing on a table in a park. <u>Curious</u> she <u>swooped</u> down <u>promptly</u> to <u>inspect</u> it. <u>Peering</u> into the pitcher, she <u>observed</u> that only a little water remained, and it was well beyond her reach. A <u>moment</u> later, she tried pecking the pitcher in an <u>effort</u> to break it. <u>Annoyed</u> at not being able to do so, she next <u>attempted</u> to knock it over. Again she failed. She <u>paused</u> to <u>stare</u> at the pitcher, trying to <u>devise</u> a plan to <u>solve</u> her problem. Then she flew to the ground and <u>seized</u> a little stone in her beak. Then, <u>clutching</u> the edge of the pitcher, she <u>balanced</u> herself and <u>tossed</u> the stone inside. Again and again she <u>tossed</u> in little stones. The water <u>gradually</u> rose in the pitcher. At last it reached the top, and the <u>shrewd</u> old bird <u>proceeded</u> to <u>quench</u> her thirst.

Lesson 14
Vocabulary

1. **sturdy** _____ / ster' dē / adj.
   synonyms: strong, solid, firm
   antonyms: feeble, flimsy, weak
   Runners need <u>sturdy</u> legs.
   A <u>sturdy</u> table won't wobble.
   The judge is a <u>sturdy</u> defender of justice.
   noun: sturdiness
   adverb: sturdily

2. **distress** _____ / di stres' / n., v.
   She was in <u>distress</u> when she lost her grandmother's ring. (n.)
   Baby's illness <u>distressed</u> Mother. (v.)
   adjective: distressing

3. **quarrel** _____ / kwärl / n., v.
   synonyms: fight, squabble, spat
   A <u>quarrel</u> is a fight with words. (n.)
   They <u>quarreled</u> over the rules of the game. (v.)
   adjective: quarrelsome

4. **prosper** _____ / pros' pər / v.
   synonyms: succeed, thrive
   Joan <u>prospered</u> by working hard.
   noun: prosperity
   adjective: prosperous

5. **taunt** _____ / tônt / n., v.
   synonyms: mock, insult, jeer (v.)
   The grasshopper <u>taunted</u> the ant for toiling. (v.)
   The little ant paid no attention to the <u>taunts</u>. (n.)

6. **jeer** _____ / jir / n., v.
   synonyms: taunt, razz
   The fans <u>jeered</u> the losing pitcher. (v.)
   <u>Jeers</u> are very unkind. (n.)

7. **counsel** _____ / koun′ səl / n., v.
   synonyms: advice (n.), advise (v.)
   The principal <u>counseled</u> us to be prompt. (v.)
   A wise person accepts good <u>counsel</u>. (n.)
   related noun: counselor
   homonym: council / koun′ səl /
   We have a student <u>council</u> to discuss school problems.

8. **summon** _____ / sum′ ən / v.
   synonym: call
   All tardy pupils were <u>summoned</u> to the principal's office.
   Pete <u>summoned</u> the courage to go into the deserted house.

9. **stern** _____ / stern / adj.
   synonyms: harsh, strict, severe
   antonyms: gentle, easygoing, kind
   The policeman gave the speeder a <u>stern</u> warning.
   homograph: stern
   The <u>stern</u> is the back part of a ship.

10. **unite** _____ / ū nīt′ / v.
    synonym: join
    Fifty states are <u>united</u> to form the United States of America.
    nouns: union, unity
    verb: unify

Lesson 14.
The Bundle of Sticks

A father of four <u>sturdy</u> sons was <u>distressed</u> because they <u>constantly</u> <u>quarreled</u> among themselves.

"This family will never <u>prosper</u> if you keep <u>taunting</u> and <u>jeering</u> at one another!" he <u>bellowed</u> <u>furiously</u>. "You must <u>cease</u> this <u>folly</u>!"

All his <u>attempts</u> to <u>discuss</u> the problem were in <u>vain</u>. To his <u>dismay</u> the <u>quarreling</u> continued. At last he <u>resolved</u> on one more <u>effort</u> to get them to <u>accept</u> his <u>counsel</u>. He <u>summoned</u> the four sons to his <u>presence</u>. He handed the oldest a bundle of sticks and <u>requested</u> him to break them. <u>Struggle</u> as hard as he would, the husky lad could not break them. At last, <u>exhausted</u> and <u>panting</u>, he gave up. The second son <u>seized</u> the bundle, tried, and failed. The third and fourth sons <u>volunteered</u> to try, but they, too, failed.

The father then untied the bundle and handed the single sticks to the sons to break. Of course, they snapped the sticks in half with little <u>effort</u>.

"<u>Observe</u>, my sons," said the father <u>sternly</u>. "If you, like the sticks, remain <u>united</u>, you will never be broken. <u>Quarrel</u> and separate, and you will surely <u>regret</u> your <u>folly</u>. In <u>unity</u> there is strength."

Lesson 15
Vocabulary

1. **dispute** _____ / di spūt' / n., v.
   synonyms: disagreement, argument (n.)
             disagree, argue (v.)
   antonyms: agreement (n.), agree (v.)
   Disputes between nations can lead to war. (n.)
   The batter disputed the umpire's call. (v.)

2. **exclaim** _____ / ek sklām' / v.
   "What a delicious pie!" she exclaimed.
   adjective: exclamatory
   related nouns: exclamation mark (!)
                  exclamation point (!)

3. **fierce** _____ / firs / adj.
   synonyms: wild, raging, terrible
   antonyms: tame, gentle
   Beasts of the jungle are fierce.
   A tiger is fiercer than a fox.
   The lion is the fiercest animal in the zoo.

4. **resist** _____ / ri zist' / v.
   synonyms: oppose, withstand
   The soldiers resisted the enemy bravely.
   A healthy body resists germs.
   noun: resistance
   adjective: resistant

5. **calm** _____ / käm / n, v., adj.
   synonyms: quiet, peaceful (adj.)
             (make) quiet (v.)
             peacefulness (n.)
   antonyms: stormy, excitable (adj.)
   The sea was calm after the storm. (adj.)
   Mother calmed the crying child. (v.)
   There is usually calm in the woods. (n.)

6. **declare** _____ / di klär′ / v.
   synonyms: say (firmly), announce
   "I won't shop in that store again," he <u>declared</u>.
   War was <u>declared</u> between the two nations.
   noun: declaration
   adjective: declarative

7. **challenge** _____ / chal′ ənj / n., v.
   synonym: dare
   Pete <u>challenged</u> me to a race. (v.)
   I accepted his <u>challenge</u> instantly. (n.)
   noun: challenger
   adjective: challenging

8. **emerge** _____ / i merj′ / v.
   The sun <u>emerged</u> from behind the clouds.
   adjective: emerging

9. **persuade** _____ / per swäd′ / v.
   synonyms: win (over), convince
   We <u>persuaded</u> Don to go with us.
   Are you <u>persuaded</u> that you can do the job?
   noun: persuasion
   adjective: persuasive

10. **triumph** _____ / trī′ əmf / n., v.
    synonyms: victory (n.), win (v.)
    antonym: defeat
    The moon landing was a <u>triumph</u> for science. (n.)
    After a hard battle, our forces <u>triumphed</u>. (v.)
    adjective: triumphant

Lesson 15.
The Wind and the Sun

An angry <u>dispute</u> arose between Wind and Sun as to which one was stronger.

"It is <u>common</u> <u>knowledge</u> that I am stronger than you," exclaimed Wind <u>indignantly</u>. "I can blow so <u>fiercely</u> that nothing can <u>resist</u> my power."

"Very well," <u>murmured</u> Sun <u>calmly</u>, "I <u>propose</u> that we have a friendly contest. Do you see that traveler <u>trudging</u> along the road? Let's <u>determine</u> who of us can <u>compel</u> him to remove his overcoat. The one who does so will be <u>declared</u> the stronger."

"I <u>accept</u> the <u>challenge!</u>" <u>retorted</u> Wind <u>promptly</u>.

"Then <u>proceed</u>," said Sun. "I'm sure you <u>prefer</u> to make the first <u>attempt</u>."

Wind <u>summoned</u> up all his great strength and blew <u>furiously</u>. The harder he blew, though, the tighter did the traveler <u>clutch</u> his overcoat. <u>Exhausted</u> at last, Wind was <u>compelled</u> to give up. He <u>glared</u> at Sun and <u>muttered</u>, "Your turn."

Sun <u>emerged</u> from behind a cloud and shone his beams down on the traveler. As he <u>gradually</u> became warmer, he took off his coat and folded it over his arm. Sun had <u>triumphed</u>.

"It's really easier to <u>persuade</u> people to do what you want than to use <u>brute</u> strength," observed Sun <u>calmly</u>.

Lesson 16
Vocabulary

1. **mischievous** _____ / mis′ chə vəs / adj.
   synonyms: naughty, playful
   A young pup is usually <u>mischievous</u>.
   nouns: mischief, mischief-maker

---

2. **thrust** _____ / thrust / n., v.
   synonym: push (in)
   He <u>thrust</u> his hands into his pockets. (v.)
   With one <u>thrust</u> of his sword, the knight cut off the dragon's head. (n.)

---

3. **victim** _____ / vik′ təm / n.
   The <u>victim</u> of the accident was taken to the hospital.
   verb: victimized

---

4. **monarch** _____ / mon′ ərk / n.
   synonym: ruler
   Queen Elizabeth is the <u>monarch</u> of Great Britain.
   related noun: monarchy

---

5. **service** _____ / sėr′ vəs / n.
Mail carriers perform an important <u>service</u>.
verb: serve
adjective: serviceable

6. **roar** _____ / rōr / n., v.
synonym: bellow
The old man <u>roared</u> at the boys to get out of his yard. (v.)
The lion's <u>roar</u> is a frightening sound. (n.)

7. **scornful** _____ / skôrn′ fəl / adj.
People may be <u>scornful</u> of simple food until they are hungry.
noun: scorn
verb: scorn

8. **rescue** _____ / res′ kū / n., v.
synonym: save (v.)
Searchers <u>rescued</u> the child who was lost in the woods. (v.)
Twenty people took part in the <u>rescue</u>. (n.)
related noun: rescuer

9. **gnaw** _____ / nô / v.
Dogs <u>gnaw</u> bones.
Mice <u>gnawed</u> through the cardboard box.

10. **captive** _____ / kap′ tiv / n.
synonym: prisoner
The pirates took their <u>captives</u> onto their ship.
related noun: captivity

Lesson 16.
The Lion and the Mouse

A mischievous mouse once scampered past a fierce, sleeping lion. The startled lion promptly thrust out his paw and pounced upon his little victim.

"Pray do not devour me, noble monarch," wailed the desperate mouse. "Some day I may be of service to you. You will never regret letting me go."

The lion roared with laughter.

"How can a feeble little fellow like you ever help me?" exclaimed the lion scornfully.

After a moment of reflection, though, the lion was persuaded to let the mouse go. Not long afterward the lion, to his dismay, was caught in the net of some hunters in the vicinity. He bellowed and roared in terror as he struggled in vain to free himself. The mouse, hearing the lion's roars of distress, ran to the rescue. With his sharp little teeth the mouse proceeded to gnaw through the ropes that held the captive:

"Thank you, my friend," panted the lion, as he emerged from the net. "You've taught me never to sneer at somebody weaker and smaller than I."

Lesson 17
Vocabulary

1. **handsome** _____ / han′ səm / adj.
   synonyms: good-looking, generous, stately, impressive
   antonyms: ugly, unsightly, unimpressive
   That actor is a handsome man.
   Aunt Lou gave me a handsome birthday present.
   The public library is a handsome building.

_____

2. **creature** _____ / kre′ chər / n.
   Every beast, bird, fish, and insect is a creature.
   Every living creature will die someday.

_____

3. **slender** _____ / slen′ dər / adj.
   synonyms: slim, thin
   antonyms: plump, stout, fat
   Peg is tall and slender.
   The willow tree has slender branches.

_____

4. **sensitive** _____ / sen′ sə tiv / adj.
   Sensitive people are easily offended.
   A dog is sensitive to high sounds.
   We should be sensitive to the needs of others.

_____

5. **scent** _____ / sent / n.
   synonyms: smell, odor, aroma
   I like the <u>scent</u> of roses.
   homonyms: sent (did send)
               cent (penny)

6. **approach** _____ / ə prōch′ / v., n.
   The children clapped as the clown <u>approached</u>. (v.)
   The car slowed as it <u>approached</u> the crossing. (v.)
   Winter is <u>approaching</u>. (v.)
   I'm happy about the <u>approach</u> of winter. (n.)
   The <u>approach</u> to the house is through the woods. (n.)

7. **brood** _____ / brüd / n., v.
   synonym: worry (v.)
   Mary <u>brooded</u> over the mistakes she made. (v.)
   The hen was followed by her <u>brood</u> of chicks. (n.)
   The Jones family has a <u>brood</u> of five children. (n.)

8. **wander** _____ / won′ dər / v.
   synonyms: roam, stray
   Tom's dog <u>wandered</u> off and was lost.
   noun: wanderer

9. **majestic** _____ / mə jes′ tik / adj.
   synonyms: grand, splendid, noble, stately
   The Rocky Mountains have <u>majestic</u> peaks.
   noun: majesty

10. **realize** _____ / rē′ ə līz / v.
    synonym: understand
    I <u>realize</u> that I must study harder.
    noun: realization

Lesson 17.
The Foolish Stag

A stag came to a clear pool of water one summer day. As he bent to quench his thirst, he peered at his reflection.

"Indeed I am a handsome fellow," he declared. "What noble antlers! I am the envy of all the woodland creatures because of them. If only I had strong, sturdy legs to match my splendid antlers! My legs are far too slender and delicate, I regret to say."

At that moment the stag's sensitive nose caught the scent of approaching hunters. The stag leaped into the air and sped away. The slender legs that he had sneered at so scornfully enabled him to get safely beyond pursuit.

Still brooding about his handsome antlers and slender legs, the stag wandered into the forest of trees with low-hanging branches. As he tossed his head back, the majestic antlers that he was so proud of got caught in the tree branches. Struggle as he might, the desperate stag could not break loose. The hunters soon emerged from behind the trees and promptly made the stag their easy victim.

"Too late!" he gasped as he perished. "I realize too late that it is my own vanity that has done me in."

Lesson 18
Vocabulary

1. **daily** _____ / dā′ lē / adj., adv., n.
   We have a daily spelling lesson. (adj.)
   Our newspaper is delivered daily. (adv.)
   Our newspaper is called a daily. (n.)

---

2. **chore** _____ / chôr / n.
   synonyms: work, job, task
   I do my chores after school.
   Washing dishes is a chore I dislike.

---

3. **graze** _____ / grāz / v.
   Cows graze daily in the pasture.
   homograph: graze (touch lightly)
   A bullet grazed the soldier's arm.

---

4. **rumor** _____ / rü′ mər / n., v.
   There's a rumor that a new school will be built here. (n.)
   It is rumored that we'll have a test tomorrow. (v.)

---

5. **savage** _____ / sav′ ij / n., adj.
   synonyms: wild, fierce, ferocious, uncivilized, cruel
   antonyms: tame, timid, gentle, civilized
   The tiger is a <u>savage</u> beast. (adj.)
   <u>Savage</u> tribes once roamed Europe. (adj.)
   A cruel, brutal person is a <u>savage</u>. (n.)

6. **weary** _____ / wir′ ē / adj.
   synonyms: tired, exhausted
   I was <u>weary</u> after a day's work.
   noun: weariness
   related adjective: wearisome

7. **companion** _____ / kəm pan′ yən / n.
   Three <u>companions</u> went with me to camp.
   noun: companionship
   adjective: companionable

8. **weapon** _____ / wep′ ən / n.
   Swords and guns are man-made <u>weapons</u>.
   Certain drugs are <u>weapons</u> against disease.

9. **deceive** _____ / dē sēv′ / v.
   synonyms: fool, mislead
   Children <u>deceive</u> each other on April Fool's Day.
   I was <u>deceived</u> into buying a lawn mower that didn't work.
   noun: deceit
   adjective: deceitful

10. **ignore** _____ / ig nôr′ / v.
    synonym: disregard
    The driver <u>ignored</u> the policeman's warning.
    Margie <u>ignored</u> Pat at the party.

Lesson 18.
The Boy Who Cried Wolf

A shepherd boy's <u>daily</u> <u>chore</u> was to watch over his father's sheep as they <u>grazed</u> on the mountainside. There had been <u>rumors</u> about the <u>presence</u> of <u>savage</u> wolves in the <u>vicinity</u>. There was fear that these <u>fierce</u> <u>creatures</u> might <u>attempt</u> to <u>pounce</u> upon a <u>plump</u> sheep and carry it off into the nearby forest to <u>devour</u> it.

The boy soon grew <u>weary</u> of his job, for he had no <u>compan-ions</u> with whom he could talk or play. He kept <u>staring</u> at the <u>village</u> far below and at the farm workers out in the fields.

One day the boy foolishly <u>devised</u> a <u>scheme</u> to get some attention. He ran down the mountain shouting, "Wolf! Wolf!"

The <u>startled</u> workers <u>instantly</u> dropped their tools, <u>seized</u> their <u>weapons</u>, and came <u>panting</u> to the <u>rescue</u>. Of course they were <u>indignant</u> when they found that the <u>mischievous</u> boy had played a trick on them. The men warned the boy <u>sternly</u> to stop his nonsense.

A few days later the boy tried his trick again. Again the men rushed to his aid. They were <u>furious</u> to find that the boy had again <u>deceived</u> them.

Then came a day when a <u>famished</u> wolf really did <u>emerge</u> from the forest. The boy screamed for help <u>desperately</u>. His <u>shrill</u> cries were in <u>vain</u>. The workers, supposing the boy was up to his old tricks, <u>ignored</u> him. Only then did the boy <u>realize</u> how stupidly he had behaved.

Lesson 19
Vocabulary

1. **product** _____ / prod′ əkt / n.
   A <u>product</u> is something made or grown.
   Cheese is a dairy <u>product</u>.
   verb: produce
   related noun: production
   adjective: productive

---

2. **fare** _____ / fãr / n., v.
   We had fine <u>fare</u> for Thanksgiving dinner. (n.)
   Bus <u>fare</u> is forty cents. (n.)
   She <u>fared</u> well in her new job. (v.)
   homonym: fair
   We want <u>fair</u> weather for our picnic. (adj.)
   Ann has <u>fair</u> skin. (adj.)
   I won a blue ribbon at the <u>fair</u>. (n.)
   Is that a <u>fair</u> price for the car? (adj.)

---

3. **dwell** _____ / dwel / v.
   synonym: live (in)
   Most people <u>dwell</u> in some kind of house.
   verb forms: dwell, dwelt, has dwelt
   noun: dwelling

---

4. **timid** _____ / tim′ id / adj.
   synonyms: shy, bashful
   antonym: bold
   Matt was too <u>timid</u> to speak to other boys. (adj.)
   noun: timidity

---

5. **bewilder** _____ / bi wil′ dər / v.
synonyms: confuse, puzzle
He was bewildered by the directions for putting the TV stand together.
noun: bewilderment
adjective: bewildering

6. **dainty** _____ / dān′ tē / adj.
This lace collar is dainty, but the other one is daintier.
She wore her daintiest dress to the party.

7. **shriek** _____ / shrēk / n., v.
synonyms: scream, yell
Nancy shrieked with fright as the big dog ran toward her. (v.)
We heard the shriek of the train whistle in the distance. (n.)

8. **dart** _____ / därt / n., v.
The mouse darted into a hole. (v.)
The robin made a dart into the bush. (n.)
The children threw darts at a target. (n.)

9. **tremble** _____ / trem′ bəl / v., n.
synonyms: shake, quiver, shiver
The leaves trembled in the breeze. (v.)
We felt a slight tremble as the train roared by. (n.)

10. **peril** _____ / per′ əl / n.
synonym: danger
The pioneers faced perils bravely.
adjective: perilous

Lesson 19.
The Town Mouse and the Country Mouse

A country mouse once <u>persuaded</u> his old friend, a town mouse, to be his guest. The country mouse made every <u>effort</u> to please his friend. He fed him peas and corn and other farm <u>products</u>. To his <u>dismay</u>, the town mouse turned up his nose at such simple <u>fare</u>.

"I <u>prefer</u> more <u>delicate</u> food," he <u>sneered</u>. "Are you not <u>weary</u> of this dull country life? Come to town and be my <u>guest</u>. I have the good <u>fortune</u> to <u>dwell</u> in a <u>splendid</u> town house. You'll be <u>delighted</u>."

The country mouse was a <u>timid</u> <u>creature</u>, but he <u>resolved</u> to <u>accept</u> his <u>companion's</u> offer. The two set out in the evening and arrived at night. The <u>glaring</u> lights and the <u>roar</u> of traffic frightened the country mouse. He <u>clutched</u> his <u>companion's</u> paw in <u>terror</u>.

"Be <u>calm</u>, my friend," <u>exclaimed</u> the town mouse. "You'll soon get used to the noise."

Inside the house they found the remains of a fine <u>feast</u> in the dining room. The town mouse <u>scampered</u> about <u>merrily</u>, acting as <u>host</u> for his <u>bewildered</u> guest. He brought him <u>dainty</u> cakes, <u>delicious</u> cheese, and other sweets.

Suddenly they heard the <u>roar</u> of a pair of <u>savage</u> dogs as they tore into the room. <u>Spying</u> the mice, they set out in hot <u>pursuit</u>.

"It's the master's dogs! Follow me!" <u>shrieked</u> the town mouse. He <u>darted</u> into a hole in the wall. The country mouse raced to safety a <u>moment</u> before the <u>fierce</u> hounds could <u>pounce</u> upon and <u>devour</u> him. <u>Trembling</u> in <u>terror</u>, the country mouse headed for the outside door.

"Goodbye, my friend," he <u>exclaimed</u>. "I'd rather eat my simple <u>fare</u> in peace than your <u>dainty</u> food in <u>constant</u> <u>peril</u>."

Lesson 20
Vocabulary

1. **flock** _____ / flok / n., v.
   synonyms: group, crowd (n.)
   Fans <u>flocked</u> to see the movie star. (v.)
   A <u>flock</u> of geese passed overhead. (n.)

---

2. **crane** _____ / krān / n., v.
   The <u>crane</u> is a long-legged wading bird. (n.)
   <u>Cranes</u> are machines used for lifting heavy things. (n.)
   We <u>craned</u> our necks to see the show better. (v.)

---

3. **utter** _____ / ut′ ər / v.
   synonym: speak
   The surprised girl could only <u>utter</u> a few words.
   Dan <u>uttered</u> a sigh of relief when he finished his work.
   noun: utterance
   homograph: utter (complete)
   The room was in <u>utter</u> confusion. (adj.)
   She was <u>utterly</u> bewildered. (adv.)

---

4. **harvest** _____ / här′ vəst / n., v.
   He expects to <u>harvest</u> wheat in August. (v.)
   <u>Harvests</u> often take place in late summer. (n.)
   nouns: harvester, harvest moon, harvest season

---

5. **crafty** _____ / kraf′ tē / adj.
   synonyms: sly, tricky
   In fables the fox is seen as a crafty fellow.
   noun: craftiness

6. **conceal** _____ / kən sēl′ / v.
   synonym: hide
   Tom concealed the box under his bed.
   I tried to conceal my disappointment when I lost the race.
   noun: concealment

7. **destroy** _____ / di stroi′ / v.
   The barn was destroyed by fire.
   nouns: destruction, destroyer
   adjective: destructive

8. **infest** _____ / in fest′ / v.
   Our poor dog is infested with fleas.
   Mosquitoes infest swamps.
   noun: infestation

9. **urge** _____ / erj / n., v.
   Our teacher urged us to go to the science fair. (v.)
   I had an urge to eat a cookie. (n.)
   adjective: urgent

10. **dispose** _____ / dis pōz′ / v.
    He disposed of his old car by selling it.
    "It's time to dispose of these old magazines," said Mother.
    adjective: disposal, disposition

Lesson 20.
The Farmer and the Stork

A farmer grew <u>weary</u> of seeing a <u>flock</u> of <u>cranes</u> <u>swoop</u> down <u>daily</u> on his corn crop and <u>utterly</u> <u>devour</u> it.

"Goodness knows I'm not <u>wealthy</u>," he <u>muttered</u>, as he <u>brooded</u> about the loss of his future <u>harvests</u>. "I will, however, soon be <u>reduced</u> to <u>utter</u> <u>poverty</u> if I do not <u>devise</u> some <u>crafty</u> <u>scheme</u> to get rid of these <u>greedy</u> <u>creatures</u>."

After some further <u>reflection</u>, the farmer <u>purchased</u> some traps at the <u>village</u> store. He <u>proceeded</u> to <u>conceal</u> them in his cornfield. When he <u>inspected</u> them next day, he found a dozen <u>captive</u> <u>cranes</u>, as well as a <u>plump</u>, well-fed stork.

"Do not kill me, sir!" <u>exclaimed</u> the <u>sleek</u> rascal. "You may <u>observe</u> that I am not one of these <u>savage</u> <u>cranes</u> that have been <u>feasting</u> on your corn crop. It is <u>common</u> <u>knowledge</u> that we <u>majestic</u> storks are <u>noble</u> birds with a <u>talent</u> for helping farmers. We <u>destroy</u> the bugs and worms that <u>infest</u> your corn fields. I <u>urge</u> you to be generous and promptly let me go."

"Sorry," <u>retorted</u> the farmer <u>calmly</u>. "Birds of a feather <u>flock</u> together, as you know. You should be more careful about the company you keep."

With that, the farmer <u>disposed</u> of the stork as well as the cranes.

Lesson 21
Vocabulary

1. **royal** _____ / roi′ əl / adj.
   synonyms: grand, noble
   The queen lives in a royal palace.
   We were given royal treatment at the party.
   noun: royalty
   adverb: royally

   ---

2. **fatal** _____ / fa′ təl / adj.
   synonyms: deadly, terrible
   Carelessness may cause a fatal accident.
   She made the fatal mistake of quitting her job.
   noun: fatality

   ---

3. **express** _____ / eks pres′ / v., adj.
   synonyms: speak, show
   She uses simple words to express her ideas. (v.)
   We express happiness by smiling. (v.)
   Express mail is delivered fast. (adj.)
   nouns: expression, expressway
   adjective: expressive

   ---

4. **sympathy** _____ / sim′ pə thē / n.
   synonym: pity
   We have sympathy for Ann, whose mother is ill.
   verb: sympathize
   adjective: sympathetic

   ---

5. **venture** _____ / ven′ chər / n., v.
   synonyms: adventure (n.), dare (v.)
   Camping was a new <u>venture</u> for Susie. (n.)
   We wouldn't <u>venture</u> to go into that deserted house. (v.)
   adjective: venturesome

6. **apparent** _____ / ə par′ ənt / adj.
   synonyms: plain, clear, obvious
   It's <u>apparent</u> that we're going to lose this game.
   adverb: apparently

7. **linger** _____ / ling′ gər / v.
   synonym: stay
   Marge <u>lingered</u> after the other guests had left the party.
   Don't <u>linger</u>! Come straight home!
   adjective: lingering

8. **miracle** _____ / mir′ ə kəl / n.
   It would be a <u>miracle</u> if the sun rose in the west.
   adjective: miraculous

9. **cautious** _____ / kô′ shəs / adj.
   synonym: careful
   antonyms: careless, reckless
   A <u>cautious</u> driver does not speed and will not take reckless
   chances.
   noun: caution

10. **bade** _____ / bad / or / bād / v.
    synonym: commanded, told, asked
    The king <u>bade</u> the knight to kneel.
    The old man <u>bade</u> his sons farewell.
    verb forms: bid, bade, has bidden

Lesson 21.
The Sick Lion

The lion, monarch of the beasts, caused the rumor to be spread that he was suffering from a fatal illness. The illness, it was said, was so severe that his royal highness would probably not survive, but perish in the near future. All beasts living in the vicinity were urged to call and express their sympathy.

The crafty fox, who was no fool, resolved after a few moments of reflection, not to be the first to venture into the monarch's presence. He lingered outside while a goat, a sheep, and a few other creatures entered.

After a few weeks, the lion apparently made a miraculous recovery. One day he emerged from his cave, paused, and glanced around. Spying the cautious fox, who was roaming in the vicinity, the lion bellowed furiously.

"Why did you ignore my royal summons?" he roared. "Why have you not been to see me as I bade you?"

"Why, your majesty," retorted the fox with a crafty smile, "I didn't want to crowd your dwelling place. I saw many tracks going into your cave, but, curiously, I have observed none coming out. It must be very crowded in there. I prefer to wait out here until there is more room in there."

Lesson 22
Mastery Test

The Vocabulary Booster lesson for today is your Mastery Test for Lessons 12–21.

☐ Prepare for the Mastery Test by reviewing your notebook pages for Lessons 12–21.

☐ Your teacher will distribute the test. Underline the word or phrase that gives the best definition of the test word. The first one is done for you.

EXAMPLE:

1. **resist** a) oppose b) accept c) remove d) fix

☐ Review the test with your teacher and class.

☐ Record your Mastery Test score on the Mastery Test Progress Chart at the back of the book.

Lesson 23
Vocabulary

1. **journey** _____ / jer′ nē / n., v.
   synonyms: trip (n.), travel (v.)
   Our neighbors <u>journeyed</u> to Europe. (v.)
   Their <u>journey</u> lasted a month. (n.)
   plural noun: journeys

   _____

2. **wilderness** _____ / wil′ dər nəs / n.
   A <u>wilderness</u> is a wild place where few people live.

   _____

3. **encounter** _____ / en koun′ tər / n., v.
   synonyms: meeting (n.), meet (v.)
   Our dog had an <u>encounter</u> with our cat. (n.)
   I <u>encountered</u> a flock of sheep on the road. (v.)

   _____

4. **solemn** _____ / sol′ əm / adj.
   The church service began with a <u>solemn</u> hymn.
   Scouts make <u>solemn</u> promises to be honest and trustworthy.
   noun: solemnity / sə lem′ nə tē /

   _____

5. **pledge** _____ / plej / n., v.
   synonyms: promise, vow
   Scouts <u>pledge</u> to be honest and loyal. (v.)
   A IOU is a <u>pledge</u> to pay what you owe. (n.)

   _____

6. **desert** _____ / di zėrt′ / v.
   synonyms: leave, forsake
   A loyal friend won't <u>desert</u> you in time of trouble.
   A ghost town has been <u>deserted</u> by everyone.
   noun: desertion
   adjective: deserted
   homonym: dessert / di zėrt′ / n.
                  We eat <u>dessert</u> after dinner.
   [Watch out for **desert** / dez′ ərt / (n.). The Sahara is a desert.]

7. **lumber** _____ / lum′ bər / v.
   synonyms: walk (heavily), go (heavily)
   The huge bear <u>lumbered</u> down the road.
   homograph: lumber / lum′ bər / (n.). pieces of wood cut for building

8. **rely** _____ / ri lī′ / v.
   synonyms: depend, trust
   We can't <u>rely</u> on the weather staying fair.
   I <u>rely</u> on Betty to do a good job.
   noun: reliance
   adjectives: reliable, reliant

9. **threaten** _____ / thret′ ən / v.
   Mother <u>threatened</u> to punish the mischievous children.
   Black clouds <u>threaten</u> rain.
   noun: threat

10. **forsake** _____ / fôr sāk′ / v.
    synonyms: leave, desert
    Don't <u>forsake</u> your good old friends.
    verb forms: forsake, forsook, has forsaken
    adjective: forsaken

Lesson 23.
The Two Young Men and a Bear

Once upon a time two young men were planning a journey through the wilderness.

"I venture to say that we shall encounter many challenging perils," declared the first young man. "We could become the victims of savage beasts seeking to devour us. We can be more secure if we resolve to stand by each other. Let us therefore make a solemn pledge to each other never to desert his companion in times of danger."

The second young man agreed, and the two shook hands solemnly. They had only gone a few miles on their perilous journey when a fierce bear caught their scent and rushed at them furiously. The first young man uttered a shrill shriek of terror. He threw their only weapon aside, leaped desperately into a tree, and clambered high into the branches. The second young man he left to rescue himself.

That second young man threw himself on the ground. He lay still as he could, for he had heard that wild creatures will not bother a dead person. The bear thrust his nose into the lad's face and sniffed curiously. As the young man was apparently dead, he lumbered off into the woods.

When he was sure the bear was gone, the first young man sprang from the tree and approached his friend.

"Wow!" he exclaimed. "That was a close one! The bear seemed to be whispering in your ear. What did the brute say?"

He laughed.

"Oh, he did speak," retorted the second young man. "He told me not to rely on a friend who will forsake you when danger threatens."

Lesson 24
Vocabulary

1. **century** _____ / sen′ chər ē / n.
   A <u>century</u> is 100 years.
   We live in the twentieth <u>century</u>.

---

2. **violent** _____ / vī′ ə lənt / adj.
   synonyms: wild, strong
   He must control his <u>violent</u> temper.
   A hurricane is a <u>violent</u> storm.
   noun: violence

---

3. **defy** _____ / di fī′ / v.
   synonym: resist
   The American colonies <u>defied</u> the English king.
   noun: defiance
   adjective: defiant

---

4. **enormous** _____ / ē nôr′ məs / adj.
   synonyms: huge, gigantic, immense
   antonyms: small, tiny, little
   Dinosaurs were <u>enormous</u> creatures.
   A cat is <u>enormous</u> compared to a tiny ant.

---

5. **sway** _____ / swā / n., v.
synonym: swing
Branches <u>sway</u> in the wind. (v.)
The <u>sway</u> of the cradle put the baby to sleep. (n.)

6. **frail** _____ / frāl / adj.
synonyms: weak, breakable, sickly
antonyms: strong, sturdy, healthy
Grandmother was a strong woman, but now she is <u>frail</u>.

7. **hardy** _____ / här' dē / adj.
synonyms: strong, sturdy
antonyms: frail, weak
Daniel Boone was a <u>hardy</u> pioneer.
noun: hardiness

8. **achieve** _____ / ə chēv' / v.
She worked hard to <u>achieve</u> her goal.
Studying will help you <u>achieve</u> better grades.
noun: achievement

9. **feat** _____ / fēt / n.
The moon landing was a great <u>feat</u>.
homonym: feet (We walk on two feet.)

10. **yield** _____ / yēld / n., v.
Good soil <u>yields</u> good crops. (v.)
Bob <u>yielded</u> his place in line to me. (v.)
The <u>yield</u> from our apple tree was two bushels. (n.)

Lesson 24.
The Oak and
the Reeds

The majestic oak had stood on the bank of a stream for more than a century. Again and again, the sturdy tree had been able to resist the fierce winds that threatened to tear it down. Then one night a violent storm began to roar. The noble oak, after defying the furious blasts so long was at last torn up by the roots. Into the stream it plunged and down the stream it floated.

The enormous oak landed on a bank of slender reeds that swayed gently in the breeze.

"Why were you frail reeds not utterly destroyed in that terrible storm last night?" exclaimed the astonished oak. "I am so hardy and you are so dainty and frail! How did you achieve this amazing feat?"

"It is apparent that you have constantly relied on your great strength against the wind," observed one of the reeds. "You have been too proud to yield. We feeble reeds have long realized that we must bow cautiously when the winds blow so furiously. We dare not venture to resist. The more severely the winds blow, the more willingly we bow—and survive."

72

Lesson 25
Vocabulary

1. **strut** _____ / strut / v.
   Roosters <u>strut</u> in the barnyard.
   The proud man held his head high and <u>strutted</u> off.

2. **elegant** _____ / el′ ə gənt / adj.
   synonyms: refined, fine, beautiful
   antonyms: crude, rough, rugged
   Cinderella's crude dress became an <u>elegant</u> gown.
   That child has <u>elegant</u> manners.

3. **fowl** _____ / foul / n.
   synonym: bird
   Quails and eagles are wild <u>fowl</u>.
   <u>Fowls</u> like ducks and geese are raised for food.
   plural noun: fowl or fowls
   homonym: foul / foul / adj.
   Garbage has a <u>foul</u> smell.
   The catcher caught the <u>foul</u> ball.

4. **display** _____ / dis plā′ / n., v.
   synonym: show, exhibit
   We'll <u>display</u> the new books in the library. (v.)
   There will be a <u>display</u> of books. (n.)

5. **brilliant** _____ / bril′ yənt / adj.
   synonyms: sparkling, bright, wonderful
   Diamonds are <u>brilliant</u> stones.
   Red is a <u>brilliant</u> color.
   She was a <u>brilliant</u> actress.
   nouns: brilliance, brilliancy

6. **glee** _____ / glē / n.
   synonym: joy, delight, merriment
   antonym: gloom
   The clown made the children laugh with glee.
   adjective: gleeful

7. **former** _____ / fôr′ mər / adj.
   synonyms: earlier, past
   In former times, cooking was done in a fireplace.
   Miss Gray is my former teacher.
   When I am offered cake or pie, I choose the former—cake.
   adverb: formerly

8. **mingle** _____ / ming′ gəl / v.
   synonym: mix
   A good host mingles with all the guests at a party.
   We make friends when we mingle with others.

9. **despise** _____ / di spīz′ / v.
   synonyms: dislike, scorn
   antonym: admire, like
   The brave knight despised cowards.
   I despise basketball, but I like football.
   adjective: despicable / des′ pik ə bəl /

10. **oblige** _____ / ə blīj′ / v.
    synonyms: compel, force
    Parents are obliged to send children to school.
    Donna obliged us by singing a song.
    verb form: obligate
    adjectives: obliged, obligated

Lesson 25.
The Vain Crow

A <u>vain</u> old crow <u>stared</u> <u>enviously</u> at the <u>handsome</u> peacocks that <u>strutted</u> about in the <u>village</u> park.

"What <u>elegant</u> <u>fowl</u>!" she <u>exclaimed</u>. "How <u>solemnly</u> and <u>majestically</u> they <u>display</u> their beautiful feathers! If only I could <u>secure</u> <u>brilliant</u> feathers like those!"

<u>Observing</u> that the peacocks had lost a few of their <u>gleaming</u> feathers, the crow <u>darted</u> about, picking them up. <u>Clutching</u> them in her claws, she began to <u>thrust</u> them among her black ones.

"There!" she cawed <u>gleefully</u>. "Now I, too, look like a <u>handsome</u> peacock."

The old crow now began to <u>ignore</u> her <u>former</u> crow friends, and <u>attempted</u> to <u>mingle</u> with the peacocks. They were not <u>deceived</u>, though. <u>Furiously</u> they yanked out her peacock feathers and drove her off.

The crow got no <u>sympathy</u> from her old <u>companions</u> when she <u>attempted</u> to rejoin them. They <u>jeered</u> at her and <u>scornfully</u> <u>taunted</u> her for having <u>deserted</u> her own kind. <u>Despised</u> by all, the poor <u>vain</u> crow was <u>obliged</u> to live alone, a <u>victim</u> of her own <u>vanity</u>.

Lesson 26
Vocabulary

1. **boast** _____ / bōst / n., v.
   synonym: brag
   Eddie boasted that he was the best football player. (v.)
   Larry's boast is that he can beat everyone else in a race. (n.)
   adjective: boastful

2. **superior** _____ / sə pir′ ē ər / adj., n.
   synonym: better (than others)
   antonym: inferior
   Nan's book report is superior to mine. (adj.)
   Lake Superior is superior to the other Great Lakes in size. (adj.)
   Mr. Blake is my superior at work. (n.)

3. **contempt** _____ / kon tempt′ / n.
   synonym: scorn
   People feel contempt for a traitor.
   adjective: contemptible

4. **signal** _____ / sig′ nəl / n., v.
   synonym: sign (n.)
   Lights on a ship signal to other ships. (v.)
   A flashing red light is a danger signal at a railroad crossing. (n.)

5. **obstinate** _____ / ob′ stə nət / adj.
   synonyms: stubborn, headstrong
   The obstinate girl would not admit she was wrong.
   adverb: obstinately

6. **determine** _____ / di tėr′ mən / v.
   synonym: decide
   Jack determined that he would become a doctor.
   The doctor determined that I didn't need glasses.
   noun: determination
   adjective: determined

7. **perform** _____ / pər fôrm′ / v.
   synonyms: do, act
   She performs her tasks willingly.
   The magician performed many tricks.
   nouns: performance, performer

8. **slumber** _____ / slum′ bər / n., v.
   synonym: sleep
   A baby's slumber is easily disturbed. (n.)
   We slumbered all morning. (v.)

9. **assemble** _____ / ə sem′ bəl / v.
   synonym: gather
   The pupils assembled for a meeting.
   Have you ever assembled a model airplane?
   noun: assembly

10. **spectator** _____ / spek′ tā tər / n.
    synonyms: watcher, bystander
    Thousands of spectators watched the baseball game.
    Spectators gathered at the scene of the accident.

Lesson 26.
The Hare and the Tortoise

Like the other forest creatures, Tortoise had grown tired of Hare's constant boasting about his superior talent as runner. Weary of Hare's scornful sneers and contempt for his own lack of ability to run, Tortoise challenged him to a race.

Hare declared himself delighted to accept. Time and place were agreed upon and the starting signal was given. Hare leaped forward, scampered off, and was out of sight in a few moments. Poor Tortoise lumbered on, obstinately determined to do his very best.

Soon Hare paused and glanced back.

"Ho, hum," he muttered. "Old Slowpoke's not yet in sight. Apparently I can take a little nap and still beat him. The spectators will have to admit that I'll have performed another one of my brilliant feats."

Hare did fall asleep. In fact, he slumbered so long that Tortoise caught up with him and passed him. Tortoise's sympathetic fans, who had assembled at the finish line, greeted him with cheers of triumph. The applause woke the startled Hare. He sprang to his feet and raced desperately in pursuit of Tortoise. He got there just in time to see Tortoise hoisted to the shoulders of his gleeful fans.

Lesson 27
Vocabulary

1. **support** _____ / sə pôrt' / n., v.
   synonym: prop
   Legs support us when we walk. (v.)
   Steel beams support a skyscraper. (v.)
   Parents support their children. (v.)
   The branches of the apple tree need support. (n.)
   The class president needs our support. (n.)
   related noun: supporter

---

2. **combat** _____ / kom' bat / n.,
                                          / kəm bat' / v.
   synonyms: fight, battle
   Doctors combat disease. (v.)
   The soldier was wounded in combat. (n.)
   related noun: combatant
   adjective: combative

---

3. **rival** _____ / rī' vəl / n., v.
   The two boys are friends, but rivals in sports. (n.)
   The stores rivaled each other in beautiful displays. (v.)
   related noun: rivalry

---

4. **refuge** _____ / ref' ūj / n.
   synonym: shelter
   The mouse took refuge in a mousehole.
   The old barn was our refuge from the rain.
   related noun: refugee

---

5. **loyal** _____ / loi′ / əl / adj.
   synonyms: faithful, true
   A <u>loyal</u> friend will stand by you in time of trouble.
   A <u>loyal</u> citizen loves his country.
   noun: loyalty

6. **empire** _____ / em′ pīr / n.
   An <u>empire</u> is a group of nations under one ruler.
   The Roman <u>Empire</u> lasted over 400 years.
   related nouns: emperor, empress

7. **talon** _____ / tal′ ən / n.
   synonym: claw
   Eagles have strong, curved <u>talons</u>.

8. **reign** _____ / rān / n., v.
   synonym: rule
   Queen Elizabeth II now <u>reigns</u> in England. (v.)
   The <u>reign</u> of Queen Victoria lasted 64 years. (n.)
   homonyms: rain and rein.
   We need <u>rain</u> for our gardens.
   He took the <u>reins</u> and guided the horse.

9. **sovereign** _____ / sov′ rən / n., adj.
   Kings and queens are <u>sovereigns</u>. (n.)
   The USA is a <u>sovereign</u>, or independent, nation of fifty states. (adj.)

10. **proclaim** _____ / prə klām / v.
    synonym: announce
    Jane was <u>proclaimed</u> the winner of the election.
    The President <u>proclaimed</u> Thanksgiving a national holiday.
    noun: proclamation

Lesson 27.
The Barnyard Monarch

Two <u>sturdy</u> roosters were locked in <u>desperate</u> <u>combat</u> to <u>determine</u> which one would become <u>monarch</u> of the barnyard. The <u>spectators</u>, the chickens, ducks, and geese, had <u>assembled</u> to give <u>vocal</u> <u>support</u> to the two <u>rivals</u>. The bitter <u>struggle</u> ended at last. The loser, having <u>yielded</u>, was <u>obliged</u> to <u>seek</u> <u>refuge</u> in a far corner of the barnyard. There he sat, <u>brooding</u> over his defeat, amid the <u>taunts</u> and <u>jeers</u> of his victorious <u>rival's</u> friends.

Amid the <u>applause</u> of his friends, the <u>triumphant</u> winner <u>strutted</u> about proudly, making <u>solemn</u> <u>pledges</u> to give <u>superior</u> <u>service</u> to his <u>loyal</u> <u>supporters</u>. A few <u>moments</u> later he flew up to the roof of the barn. There he cawed and flapped his wings <u>furiously</u> so that all <u>fowls</u> in the <u>vicinity</u> would <u>realize</u> who would <u>reign</u> over the barnyard <u>empire</u> in the <u>future</u>.

In fact, he made so much noise that a passing eagle <u>spied</u> him, <u>swooped</u> down, and <u>seized</u> him in his <u>talons</u>. He carried his helpless <u>victim</u> off to his nest to feed his young ones.

Meanwhile, the defeated rooster <u>emerged</u> from his hiding place and <u>modestly</u> <u>proclaimed</u> himself the new <u>royal</u> <u>sovereign</u> of the barnyard.

Lesson 28
Vocabulary

1. **distract** _____ / dis trakt' / v.
   synonym: disturb
   Noise distracts me when I'm studying.
   noun: distraction

   _____

2. **nymph** _____ / nimf / n.
   In old tales, nymphs were beautiful girls who never grew old.
   Today, we call a very young insect a nymph.

   _____

3. **occupy** _____ / ok' yə pī / v.
   Two families occupy that house.
   Dave is occupied with basketball practice.
   The President occupies an important position.
   nouns: occupant, occupancy

   _____

4. **chatter** _____ / chat' ər / n., v.
   synonym: talk
   The girls chattered about the party. (v.)
   There was a lot of chatter about the party. (n.)
   related words: chat, chit-chat
   adjective: chatty

   _____

5. **gossip** _____ / gos' ip / n., v.
   Some people gossip about their neighbors. (v.)
   Gossip spreads many false stories. (n.)
   noun: gossiper
   adjective: gossipy

   _____

6. **wed** _____ / wed / v.
synonym: marry
My parents were wed in New York.
nouns: wedding, wedlock
adjective: wedded

7. **image** _____ / im′ ij / n.
synonym: likeness
You see your image in a mirror.
Tom is the image of his father.
There is an image of George Washington in front of our City Hall.

8. **affair** _____ / ə fãr′ / n.
synonyms: business, happening
The principal takes care of school affairs.
The party was a grand affair.

9. **hover** _____ / huv′ ər / v.
synonym: stay (nearby)
Sea gulls hover above the water.
I don't want anyone hovering about me when I'm studying.
My dog hovers near the kitchen at mealtime.

10. **mute** _____ / mūt / adj.
synonyms: speechless, silent
Helen Keller was a mute woman who learned to speak.
John remained mute rather than admit that he didn't know the answer.

Lesson 28.
Echo and Narcissus

Hera, queen of the Greek gods, kept a sharp eye on Zeus, her <u>royal</u> husband and <u>reigning</u> <u>sovereign</u> of the gods. Once Zeus, wishing to <u>distract</u> Hera, <u>persuaded</u> Echo, a <u>dainty</u> young <u>nymph</u>, to keep Hera <u>occupied</u> while the <u>crafty</u> <u>monarch</u> did as he pleased. Echo <u>performed</u> her <u>chore</u> brilliantly by <u>chattering</u> <u>merrily</u> about woodland <u>gossip</u> and <u>rumors</u> of love <u>affairs</u>. Hera became <u>annoyed</u> at last and <u>realized</u> she was being <u>deceived</u>. Hera was <u>furious</u>.

"I'll stop that big mouth of yours forever," she <u>proclaimed</u> <u>indignantly</u>. "You may never <u>utter</u> your own words again. You may only repeat the words of others."

Poor Echo! She had been <u>determined</u> to <u>wed</u> the <u>handsome</u> youth Narcissus. But the <u>vain</u> fellow <u>apparently</u> had eyes only for himself. <u>Strutting</u> proudly through the woods, he had <u>spied</u> his <u>image</u> in a woodland pool. <u>Astonished</u> by his own beauty, he <u>lingered</u> there day after day, <u>staring</u> constantly at his <u>reflection</u>. Echo could only <u>hover</u> <u>loyally</u> nearby and gaze at him <u>mutely</u>.

"Ah, but you are <u>handsome</u>!" Narcissus would <u>murmur</u>, <u>staring</u> at his <u>reflection</u>.

"<u>Handsome</u>," repeated Echo.

"I can love only you," <u>exclaimed</u> Narcissus.

"Only you," Echo was <u>obliged</u> to repeat.

Narcissus' strength <u>gradually</u> faded away. He <u>obstinately</u> refused to <u>pause</u> a few <u>moments</u> for food or <u>slumber</u>. One morning Echo and the other <u>nymphs</u> <u>assembled</u> and found in his place by the pool a <u>frail</u>, <u>delicate</u> flower <u>swaying</u> in the breeze. They called it the narcissus, a name it bears to this day.

Echo, too, grew even more <u>feeble</u>, pale and <u>slender</u>. At last all that remained of her was her voice. When you are out in the hills, shout into the distance. The breeze will seem to carry your voice back to you. Could it be the <u>nymph</u> Echo repeating your words as the Greek goddess Hera had demanded?

Lesson 29
Vocabulary

1. **fickle** _____ / fik′ əl / adj.
   synonym: changeable
   antonyms: loyal, constant
   A <u>fickle</u> friend may desert you suddenly.
   The weather is <u>fickle</u> lately, always changing.

---

2. **transform** _____ / trans fôrm′ / v.
   synonym: change
   Caterpillars are <u>transformed</u> into butterflies.
   noun: transformation

---

3. **damsel** _____ / dam′ zəl / n.
   synonym: girl, maiden
   <u>Damsel</u> actually means "little lady."

---

4. **flee** _____ / flē / v.
   People <u>flee</u> from danger.
   The family <u>fled</u> from the burning house.
   verb forms: flee, fled, has fled
   homonym: flea / flē /
   My poor dog has <u>fleas</u>.

---

5. **panic** _____ / pan′ ik / n., v.
   A fire can cause <u>panic</u> in a crowd. (n.)
   "Don't <u>panic</u>," said Mr. Long. "Stay calm." (v.)
   verb forms: panic, panicked, panicking

6. **impulse** _____ / im′ puls / n.
   Acting on <u>impulse</u> can lead to trouble.
   Betty had the <u>impulse</u> to step in a rain puddle.
   adjective: impulsive
   adverb: impulsively

7. **embrace** _____ / em brās′ / n., v.
   synonyms: hug, include
   Grandmother gave Nancy a loving <u>embrace</u>. (n.)
   The little girl ran to her mother and <u>embraced</u> her. (v.)
   North America <u>embraces</u> Canada, Mexico, and the United States. (v.)

8. **instinct** _____ / in′ stinkt / n.
   Birds fly south in winter by <u>instinct</u>.
   By <u>instinct</u> people jump back from danger.
   adjective: instinctive

9. **alert** _____ / ə lert′ / n., v., adj.
   synonyms: wide-awake, watchful (adj.)
              warn (v.), warning (n.)
   Lifeguards must always be <u>alert</u>. (adj.)
   Flashing red lights <u>alert</u> drivers to danger. (v.)
   Drivers should pay attention to an <u>alert</u>. (n.)

10. **constellation** _____ / kon′ stə lā′ shən / n.
    A <u>constellation</u> is a star group.
    The Big Dipper is a <u>constellation</u>.

Once upon a time Zeus, that fickle sovereign of the Greek gods, fell in love with a nymph named Callisto. When Hera, the monarch's wife, heard the rumors and gossip about Zeus's love affair, she was furious. While Zeus was otherwise distracted, she craftily transformed the sensitive young damsel into a fierce, savage bear. Callisto, who had loved to hunt, was now obliged to flee in panic whenever she encountered hunters. Zeus, unwilling to defy the obstinate Hera openly and wanting to avoid a bitter quarrel, cautiously resolved not to display his anger at the moment.

The years passed. Then one day Callisto spied a handsome young hunter wandering in her vicinity in search of game. As she stared at him, she suddenly realized that he was her own son, Arcas, now grown up. Yielding to a tender impulse, she lumbered from her hiding place to embrace him. Arcas instinctively raised his bow to send a fatal arrow into the chest of the approaching bear.

Zeus, ever alert and now inspired by pity, promptly swept both mother and son up into the heavens. There Callisto became the Big Bear, which we frequently call the Big Dipper, or Ursa Major. Arcas, united with his mother, became the Little Bear, or Little Dipper and Ursa Minor. You may observe these brilliant constellations gleaming all the year round as they proudly occupy their places in the sky.

Lesson 30
Vocabulary

1. **agriculture** _____ / ag′ rə kul′ chər / n.
   synonym: farming
   <u>Agriculture</u> is the world's most important business.
   adjective: agricultural

---

2. **vegetation** _____ / vej′ ə tā′ shən / n.
   synonym: plant
   There is not much <u>vegetation</u> in the desert.
   noun: vegetable

---

3. **adore** _____ / ə dôr′ / v.
   synonym: love
   antonyms: hate, despise
   Susie really <u>adores</u> her grandfather.
   Pete says he <u>hates</u> carrots and <u>loves</u> spinach.
   noun: adoration
   adjective: adorable

---

4. **chariot** _____ / char′ ē ət / n.
   In ancient days, a <u>chariot</u> was a two-wheeled carriage pulled by horses.
   noun: charioteer

---

5. **steed** _____ / stēd / n.
synonyms: horse, charger
The chariot was pulled by two <u>steeds</u>.

6. **famine** _____ / fam' ən / n.
A <u>famine</u> is a time when there is little food.
Millions have died in <u>famines</u> throughout history.

7. **interfere** _____ / in' tər fir' / v.
synonyms: meddle, bother, disturb
Don't <u>interfere</u> in my business.
Noise <u>interferes</u> with my studying.
Rain has <u>interfered</u> with our picnic plans.
noun: interference

8. **pomegranate** _____ / pom' gran' it / n.
The <u>pomegranate</u> tree has been known to people for thousands of years.

9. **descend** _____ / di send' / v.
synonym: fall
antonym: rise, ascend
Rain <u>descends</u> from the sky.
Rivers <u>descend</u> to the sea.
nouns: descent, descendent

10. **ascend** _____ / ə send' / v.
synonym: rise
antonym: fall, descend
Smoke <u>ascends</u> in a chimney.
The plane <u>ascended</u> and disappeared in the clouds.
nouns: ascent, ascension

Lesson 30.
Zeus Gives the Seasons

Roman Ceres, called Demeter by the ancient Greeks, was goddess of agriculture and vegetation. Ceres adored her daughter Proserpine, whom the Greeks knew as Persephone.

Once while Ceres was on a long journey, Proserpine and her friends, the nymphs, were chattering merrily as they gathered flowers in the fields. Suddenly Pluto, the Greek's Hades, god of the underworld, appeared in their midst. The damsels shrieked in terror as the underworld sovereign roared up in a chariot drawn by four enormous black steeds. Spying the dainty Proserpine, the god promptly fell in love with her. Impulsively he leaped from his chariot, seized the startled girl, and fled as she struggled vainly in his embrace.

When Ceres returned, she was overcome with grief and panic. Apparently nobody dared tell her what happened. The distracted Ceres now obstinately refused to perform her daily chores. The plants, infested by insects, dried up. The rains ceased. The crops and harvests failed, and the people were threatened with droughts and famine. Zeus, who had been unwilling to interfere, now took charge.

"The rules are clear," he proclaimed. "Proserpine has been carried off as a captive to Pluto's underworld empire. If she has slept and eaten meals there, she must remain. If not, she must be united with her mother."

It turned out that Proserpine, unwilling to eat, had finally swallowed a half dozen pomegranate seeds.

"Very well," declared Zeus. "Proserpine shall remain with Pluto for six months of the year. The other six months she will spend with Ceres. So be it."

And so, when the weather grows cold and the plants cease to grow, we realize that Proserpine has once more descended into Pluto's empire. When we observe that the farmers are planting their crops and the leaves are turning green, Proserpine has again ascended to earth to transform it miraculously into an agricultural wonderland.

Lesson 31
Vocabulary

1. **archer** _____ / är′ chər / n.
   synonym: bowman
   Robin Hood was a skilled archer.
   noun: archery

---

2. **quiver** _____ / kwiv′ ər / n.
   Archers keep their arrows in a quiver.
   homograph: quiver (tremble, shake)

---

3. **beware** _____ / bi wãr′ / v.
   Beware of skating on thin ice.
   Beware how you use a sharp knife.
   Beware lest you wake the baby.

---

4. **implore** _____ / im plôr′ / v.
   synonym: beg
   She implored her friends to help her find her lost kitten.

---

5. **sprout** _____ / sprout / n., v.
   synonyms: grow (v.), shoot (n.)
   Weeds <u>sprouted</u> in the garden. (v.)
   Rabbits like to eat the tiny <u>sprouts</u> of beans. (n.)

6. **respond** _____ / ri spond' / v.
   synonyms: answer, reply
   "Yes, I'll help you," Beth <u>responded</u>.
   No one could <u>respond</u> to the teacher's question.
   Our dog <u>responds</u> to strangers by barking.
   noun: response
   adjective: responsive

7. **plea** _____ / plē / n.
   The hungry child made a <u>plea</u> for food.
   Ms. Hill drove through a red light. Her <u>plea</u> was that she did not see it.
   verb: plead

8. **laurel** _____ / lôr' əl / n.
   The <u>laurel</u> is an evergreen shrub with dark, glossy leaves.
   Wreaths are sometimes made with <u>laurel</u> leaves.

9. **wreath** _____ / rēth / n.
   Christmas <u>wreaths</u> are often made of holly.
   A <u>wreath</u> of flowers was put on the hero's grave.
   verb: wreathe / rē<u>th</u> /

10. **symbol** _____ / sim' bəl / n.
    The eagle is the <u>symbol</u> of the United States.
    verb: symbolize
    homonym: cymbal / sim' bəl / n.
    <u>Cymbals</u> are used in orchestras.

Lesson 31.
Apollo's Laurel Wreath

Handsome Apollo, the sun god, was the son of Zeus, monarch of all the Greek gods. It was Apollo who drove his gleaming sun chariot daily across the skies. He was also a brilliant archer, famed for his skill with bow and arrow.

Eros, whom the Romans knew as Cupid, was the mischievous son of Aphrodite, goddess of love and beauty. He, too, was an archer. When he sped one of his tiny golden arrows into people's hearts, they promptly fell in love with the ones they happened to be looking at at the moment. But Eros kept lead arrows in his quiver, too. The lead arrows inspired hate, though, instead of love.

One day Apollo chanced to encounter little Eros. The sun god boasted about his superior weapons and began to jeer and taunt the little fellow.

"Beware!" exclaimed Eros, glaring furiously at his rival. "I may give you reasons to regret your insults!"

The little rascal kept his word. Spying Apollo gossiping merrily with Daphne, daughter of a river god, he popped a tiny arrow into his heart. An instant later he sped a lead dart into the damsel's breast.

Of course, Apollo promptly fell in love with the nymph, and she, in turn, instinctively began to despise the handsome god.

"I adore you!" exclaimed Apollo, as he impulsively sought to embrace her. Daphne, shrieking in terror, fled as Apollo pursued her. Desperately she implored her father, the river god, to rescue her. Suddenly her dainty feet took root. Bark sprouted from her body. The river god had responded to her pleas by transforming her into a laurel tree!

The startled Apollo finally realized what had happened. He proclaimed the laurel to be HIS tree and wove the leaves into a wreath. Apollo's laurel wreath has been used throughout the centuries as a symbol of victory for contest winners.

1. **maiden** _____ / mād′ ən / n., adj.
   synonyms: girl, damsel
   Many <u>maidens</u> loved the handsome prince. (n.)
   The ship Titantic sank on its <u>maiden</u> voyage. (adj.)
   Mother's <u>maiden</u> name was Mildred Jones. (adj.)
   related noun: bridesmaid
   related adjective: maidenly

2. **flatter** _____ / flat′ ər / v.
   Joe <u>flattered</u> his boss to try to get ahead.
   The boss knew very well that Joe was <u>flattering</u> him.
   Some pictures <u>flatter</u> a person.
   nouns: flattery, flatterer

3. **object** _____ / ob′ jikt / n.
   / əb jekt′ / v.
   synonyms: thing, goal, purpose (n.), oppose (v.)
   A pin is a small <u>object</u>. (n.)
   Her <u>object</u> is to be elected president. (n.)
   My <u>object</u> in coming was to see the display. (n.)
   Some dogs <u>object</u> to a bath. (v.)
   related nouns: objection, objective

4. **reluctant** _____ / ri luk′ tənt / adj.
   synonym: unwilling
   antonym: eager, willing
   A miser is <u>reluctant</u> to spend his money.
   noun: reluctance
   adverb: reluctantly

5. **persist** _____ / pər sist′ / v.
   synonyms: continue, stay
   My family <u>persists</u> in calling me by my nickname.
   The rain <u>persisted</u> all week.
   noun: persistence
   adjective: persistent

6. **dispatch** _____ / dis pach′ / n., v.
   synonyms: message, speed (n.), send (v.)
   Food was <u>dispatched</u> to the flood victims. (v.)
   Reporters send <u>dispatches</u> to their newspapers. (n.)
   Mike works with neatness and <u>dispatch</u>.
   [Another spelling of dispatch is despatch.]

7. **remorse** _____ / ri môrs′ / n.
   The thief felt <u>remorse</u> over his crime.
   adjectives: remorseful, remorseless

8. **weep** _____ / wēp / v.
   synonyms: cry, sob
   Peg is <u>weeping</u> because she lost her ring.
   Larry <u>wept</u> when his dog ran away.
   Sometimes people <u>weep</u> for joy.
   verb forms: weep, wept, has wept

9. **despair** _____ / di spār′ / n., v.
   synonym: hopelessness (n.)
   The woman wept in <u>despair</u> when her son died. (n.)
   I <u>despaired</u> of ever finding my money. (v.)

10. **gloomy** _____ / glüm′ ē / adj.
    synonyms: sad, blue, downcast, dark, dreary
    antonyms: cheery, cheerful, jolly, sunny
    Matt is <u>gloomy</u> because he is lonesome.
    I like <u>sunny</u> days better than <u>gloomy</u> days.
    Monday was <u>gloomier</u> than Sunday.
    Monday was the <u>gloomiest</u> day of the week.
    noun: gloom

Lesson 32.
Apollo and Coronis

Apollo had another unhappy love affair. A fickle maiden named Coronis was naturally flattered to be the object of the handsome sun monarch's attention. She was reluctant, though, to desert a young man whom she had long adored. She persisted obstinately in meeting him frequently, in spite of Apollo's pleas and violent threats.

Now Apollo had a loyal servant, an elegant white fowl, a raven. This bird, like her cousins, the crows, had brilliant, gleaming white feathers. Apollo's alert raven got into the habit of spying on Coronis and her companion. Once, having observed them embracing, she flew back, shrieking indignantly to tell Apollo what she had seen.

The furious Apollo, responding promptly, despatched an arrow in the direction of the lovers. The fatal dart struck Coronis instead of Apollo's rival, however. Filled with remorse for his impulsive act, Apollo broke down and wept bitterly.

In utter despair, he now sternly declared that his raven's white feathers must be transformed into black ones. The bird was to leave his service and dwell with Pluto in the future, in the underworld sovereign's gloomy empire.

And so, say the ancient Greek myths, all ravens and crows are now black instead of white.

Lesson 33
Mastery Test

The Vocabulary Booster lesson for today is your Mastery Test for Lessons 23–32.

☐ Prepare for the Mastery Test by reviewing your notebook pages for Lessons 23–32.

☐ Your teacher will distribute the test. Underline the word or phrase that gives the best definition of the test word. The first one is done for you.

EXAMPLE:

1. **strut** a) <u>walk proudly</u> b) stray behind c) crow
   d) wander

☐ Review the test with your teacher and class.

☐ Record your Mastery Test score on the Mastery Test Progress Chart at the back of the book.

Lesson 34
Vocabulary

1. **gaze** _____ / gāz / n., v.
   synonym: look
   She gazed at the lovely clothes in the shop. (v.)
   He gave the baby a loving gaze.

2. **haughty** _____ / hôt′ ē / adj.
   synonyms: vain, conceited
   antonym: humble
   A haughty person thinks he is better than others.
   Both girls are haughty, but Alice is the haughtier.
   Sam is the haughtiest boy on the team.

3. **aware** _____ / ə wār′ / adj.
   synonym: knowing
   I was not aware of my mistake.
   Are you aware that this is your third test word?
   noun: awareness

4. **dusk** _____ / dusk / n.
   We stayed outdoors until dusk.
   It is cool in the dusk of the forest.
   adjective: dusky

5. **dawn** _____ / dôn / n., v.
   Roosters crowed at <u>dawn.</u> (n.)
   A fine idea has <u>dawned</u> on me. (v.)

6. **resume** _____ / ri zŭm′ / v.
   We'll <u>resume</u> the lesson after recess.
   Mrs. Smith <u>resumed</u> her job as a school nurse.
   noun: résumé / rez′ ü mā /

7. **vigil** _____ / vij′ əl / n.
   synonym: watch
   Doctors kept a <u>vigil</u> over the sick child.
   nouns: vigilance, vigilante / vij′ i lan′ tē /
   adjective: vigilant

8. **disk** _____ / disk / n.
   Dimes and nickels and other coins are <u>disks</u>.
   I have a <u>disk</u> of band music for my record player.
   [We can also spell disk disc.]

9. **consist** _____ / kən sist′ / v.
   A year <u>consists</u> of fifty-two weeks.
   This lesson <u>consists</u> of ten new words.
   noun: consistency
   adjective: consistent
   adverb: consistently

10. **feminine** _____ / fem′ ə nən / adj.
    synonyms: womanly, dainty
    antonym: masculine
    Julie sang in a high <u>feminine</u> voice and her brother sang in a deep
    <u>masculine</u> voice.
    A delicate lace hanky is a <u>feminine</u> object.

Lesson 34.
Apollo and the Sunflower

Apparently the handsome Apollo's good looks did not inspire the love of Daphne or Coronis. On the other hand, most Greek damsels responded eagerly whenever he spoke to them, for he had a host of feminine admirers. Among the most loyal was a slender maiden name Clytie. Each morning Apollo summoned his hardy white steeds for his daily journey through the skies. From the time he clambered into his chariot until he disappeared in the western heavens, Clytie never ceased to gaze mutely at him. All the day long she obstinately persisted in keeping her adoring eyes fixed on the majestic object of her love.

But, sad to say, the haughty monarch of the skies never even became aware of her presence. Day after day he calmly ignored her imploring glances.

Poor Clytie! She would not pause to eat or quench her thirst. At dusk, weary and exhausted, she fell into despairing slumber. But every dawn she rose promptly to resume her vigil. Gradually she grew more feeble and frail. When she was almost at the point of perishing, the gods decided that it was time to interfere. They assembled to express their sympathy and to discuss what they might do to help her.

And help her they did! They transformed her from the timid maiden into—a sunflower! The new sunflowers consisted of flat disks as much as seventeen inches wide. They grew on sturdy stalks that rose to fifteen feet high. The gods ringed the disks with heart-shaped leaves to serve as symbols of Clytie's love for Apollo. Now when the sun travels across the sky between dawn and dusk, the flower disks crane their slender necks and turn slowly in order to keep facing the sun.

Lesson 35
Vocabulary

1. **ridicule** ———————————— / rid′ ə kūl / n., v.
   synonym: taunt
   antonym: praise
   The haughty woman ridiculed her neighbor's poor clothes. (v.)
   Silly behavior brings ridicule on a person. (n.)

2. **appeal** ———————————— / ə pēl′ / n., v.
   synonyms: plea, request (n.)
             beg, ask, plead (v.)
   Pete appealed to his sister for help. (v.)
   Pete made an appeal for help. (n.)
   Does ice cream appeal to you? (v.)
   It has appeal for most people. (n.)

3. **sacred** ———————————— / sā krəd / adj.
   synonym: holy
   Temples and churches are sacred buildings.
   The knight made a sacred vow to do his duty.

4. **oath** ———————————— / ōth / n.
   The witness took an oath to tell the truth.
   The angry man muttered an oath.

5. **grant** _____ / grant / n., v.
   synonyms: give, admit (v.); gift (n.)
   The prisoner was <u>granted</u> freedom. (v.)
   I <u>grant</u> that you are the better swimmer. (v.)
   The settlers each received a <u>grant</u> of land. (n.)

6. **soar** _____ / sôr / v.
   An eagle <u>soared</u> in the sky.
   The price of meat is soaring.
   homonym: sore / sôr / n. adj.
   My <u>sore</u> throat hurts. (adj.)
   The <u>sore</u> on my leg is healing. (n.)

7. **summit** _____ / sum′ it / n.
   synonyms: top, peak
   Snow remains on the <u>summits</u> of high mountains.

8. **instantly** _____ / in′ stənt lē / adv.
   synonym: immediately
   They stopped talking <u>instantly</u>.
   noun: instant
   adjective: instant

9. **hurl** _____ / hėrl / v.
   synonyms: throw, pitch
   The boxes were <u>hurled</u> from the truck.
   Pitchers <u>hurl</u> baseballs.
   noun: hurler

10. **create** _____ / krē āt′ / v.
    The artist <u>created</u> a beautiful painting.
    Traffic <u>creates</u> noise in the city.
    Music <u>creates</u> a lot of pleasure for us.

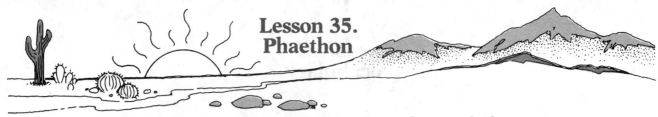

Lesson 35.
Phaethon

Apollo was once wedded to a nymph named Clymene. They had a son whom they called Phaethon. The boy never got much attention from his father, who was occupied from dawn to dusk in performing his chores.

"Are you aware," the haughty Phaethon would boast to his friends, "that I am the son of the great Apollo?"

The boy's companions soon ceased to believe him. Phaethon became an object of contempt and ridicule. Weeping in despair, the boy in desperation appealed to his mother. She impulsively counseled the lad to request his father to help him. He resolved to do so and ventured the long journey to Apollo's stables.

Apollo was delighted to see the boy.

"Of course you are truly my son," he roared indignantly. "What can I do to persuade your friends who you are? I swear the sacred oath of the gods that I will grant you any wish. I solemnly swear by the River Styx in Hades."

It was common knowledge that swearing by the River Styx bound the gods to any pledge they made. The boy's eyes gleamed.

"Then let me drive your great chariot!" exclaimed Phaethon. "I implore you, father!"

"Beware, my son," said the sun monarch sternly, frowning in dismay. "You propose a favor that I cannot grant. Only I can control those enormous steeds. You will destroy yourself. It would be utter folly!"

But the obstinate boy persisted in his plea. At last Apollo was compelled to keep his word. The boy clambered into the chariot and seized the reins. The steeds leaped into the air. High over the earth they soared, leaving icy mountain summits behind. As they plunged too close to the earth, they left burned-out vegetation and long stretches of desert.

Zeus, watching from afar, was obliged to interfere. Instantly he hurled one of his deadly thunderbolts at the wildly swaying chariot. The bewildered Phaethon plunged to his death.

Now, when you gaze at the majestic frozen summits of the mountains or at our desert wilderness, remember that it was Phaethon, the son of Apollo, who created them.

Lesson 36
Vocabulary

1. **attract** _____ / ə trakt' / v.
   synonym: pull (toward)
   Magnets <u>attract</u> metals like iron and steel.
   Bees are <u>attracted</u> to flowers.
   Her beauty <u>attracted</u> all eyes.
   noun: attraction
   adjective: attractive

2. **eternal** _____ / ē tėr' nəl / adj.
   synonyms: everlasting, endless
   Life on earth is not <u>eternal</u>; all plants and animals die someday.
   noun: etern ty

3. **limb** _____ / lim / n.
   synonym: branch
   The oak tree has a large broken <u>limb</u>.
   Human beings have four <u>limbs</u>, two legs and two arms.

4. **neglect** _____ / nə glekt' / n., v.
   Mac <u>neglected</u> his health and became ill. (v.)
   Don't <u>neglect</u> your homework. (v.)
   The poor thin dog is suffering from <u>neglect</u>. (n.)
   adjectives: neglected, neglectful

5. **charm** _____ / chärm / n., v.
   synonym: please (v.)
   A baby's smile <u>charms</u> people. (v.)
   A thoughtful person has <u>charm</u> for me. (n.)
   I want a bracelet with silver <u>charms</u>. (n.)
   The fairy godmother used her wand as a <u>charm</u> to put a spell on the queen. (n.)
   adjective: charming

6. **abandon** _____ / ə ban′ dən / v.
   synonyms: desert, forsake
   The sailors <u>abandoned</u> the sinking ship. (v.)

7. **odd** _____ / od / adj.
   synonyms: funny, strange, curious, left-over
   A jellyfish has an <u>odd</u> shape.
   I heard an <u>odd</u> noise at the window.
   Numbers 1, 3, 5, 7, and 9 are <u>odd</u> numbers.
   I have three socks, one pair and one <u>odd</u> sock.
   noun: oddity

8. **vigor** _____ / vig′ ər / n.
   synonyms: strength, health, force
   Young athletes are full of <u>vigor</u>.
   Peg speaks with <u>vigor</u> for what she believes.
   adjective: vigorous

9. **fling** _____ / fling / v.
   synonym: throw
   Don't <u>fling</u> your coat on a chair.
   The tired girl <u>flung</u> herself across the bed.
   verb forms: fling, flung, has flung

10. **mortal** _____ / môr′ təl / n., adj.
    antonym: immortal (adj.)
    Everyone is <u>mortal</u> and will die someday. (adj.)
    No human being is <u>immortal</u>. (adj.)
    The soldier received a <u>mortal</u> wound. (adj.)
    No <u>mortal</u> will live forever on this earth. (n.)

Lesson 36.
Tithonus

The Greek gods <u>frequently</u> had love affairs with <u>mortal</u> <u>maidens</u>. The goddesses, too, were sometimes <u>attracted</u> to <u>handsome</u>, <u>mortal</u> men and might even <u>wed</u> them. Once Aurora, the <u>dainty</u> Roman goddess of the <u>dawn</u>, became the <u>victim</u> of one of <u>mischievous</u> Cupid's golden <u>darts</u>. She fell hopelessly in love with Tithonus, a prince of Troy, and a <u>mortal</u>.

Aurora, who <u>flung</u> open the heavenly gates for Apollo's <u>steeds</u> to begin their <u>daily</u> <u>journey</u>, <u>implored</u> the gods to <u>grant</u> <u>eternal</u> life to her <u>mortal</u> lover. The gods were <u>sympathetic</u>, but were hard to <u>persuade</u>. At last they <u>reluctantly</u> granted Aurora's <u>persistent</u> <u>request</u>. She was <u>delighted</u> and <u>promptly</u> <u>wed</u> the young man.

The years passed. To her growing <u>dismay</u>, Aurora became <u>aware</u> that her beloved Tithonus was growing old! His voice became <u>shrill</u>. His eyes grew dim. He grew bald and lost his teeth. The once <u>hardy</u> prince <u>gradually</u> grew more <u>frail</u> and <u>feeble</u>. His formerly <u>sturdy</u> <u>limbs</u> began to <u>quiver</u> and <u>tremble</u> as he grew weaker.

Poor Aurora! She now realized that she had <u>neglected</u> to <u>plead</u> for <u>eternal</u> youth when she had <u>secured</u> <u>eternal</u> life. Aurora, of course, lost none of her <u>delicate</u> <u>feminine</u> charms as she grew older, for she, like other gods, enjoyed the gift of <u>eternal</u> youth. True to her <u>sacred</u> <u>wedding</u> <u>oath</u>, she refused to <u>abandon</u> Tithonus. The gods, again <u>sympathetic</u>, <u>assembled</u> to <u>discuss</u> what they might do to help. They came up with an <u>odd</u> answer. They <u>transformed</u> Tithonus into—a grasshopper! Aurora could <u>cease</u> the <u>weary</u> chore of nursing him, and the old fellow was <u>enabled</u> to <u>leap</u> and <u>soar</u> with all the <u>vigor</u> of his <u>former</u> active youth.

And so, say the <u>ancient</u> myths, when you see a lively grasshopper <u>leaping</u> about, remember that he is Tithonus, the elderly husband of Aurora, the goddess of <u>dawn</u>.

Lesson 37
Vocabulary

1. **fond** _____ / fond / adj.
   synonym: loving
   Mother gave the baby a <u>fond</u> smile.
   expression: be fond of (like a lot)
   Most people are <u>fond</u> of ice cream.
   noun: fondness
   adverb: fondly

---

2. **huge** _____ / hūj / adj.
   synonyms: large, enormous, tremendous
   antonyms: tiny, little, small
   We ate a <u>huge</u> Thanksgiving dinner.
   The elephant is a <u>huge</u> animal.
   Sally is wearing a <u>huge</u> straw hat.

---

3. **reveal** _____ / ri vēl' / v.
   synonyms: show, display
   antonyms: conceal, hide
   The map <u>revealed</u> where the treasure was buried.
   A smile <u>reveals</u> happiness.
   Please don't <u>reveal</u> my secret.
   noun: revelation

---

4. **caress** _____ / kə res' / n., v.
   synonyms: pet, hug
   Jennie gave her little sister a fond <u>caress</u>. (n.)
   Bob <u>caressed</u> the kitten gently. (v.)

---

5. **heifer** _____ / hef′ ər / n.
The farmers herd consists of bulls, cows, <u>heifers</u>, and a few calves.

6. **favorite** _____ / fāv′ ə rit / n., adj.
Of all flowers, the rose is my <u>favorite</u>. (n.)
Tom's <u>favorite</u> food is a hamburger. (adj.)
verb: favor

7. **hesitate** _____ / hez′ ə tāt / v.
Always <u>hesitate</u> before crossing a busy street.
I <u>hesitated</u> to answer because I wasn't sure what to say.
noun: hesitation
adjective: hesitant

8. **sentry** _____ / sen′ trē / n.
synonyms: watchman, guard, sentinel
A <u>sentry</u> stood outside the palace gate.
A <u>sentry</u> walked up and down at the entrance to the fort.

9. **falter** _____ / fôl′ tər / v.
synonyms: hesitate, stumble
The courage of the soldiers did not <u>falter</u>.
The sick man <u>faltered</u> from weakness.
The boy <u>faltered</u> when he replied because he didn't know the answer.

10. **forlorn** _____ / fôr lôrn′ / adj.
synonyms: lonesome, lonely, sad
The lost puppy was sick and <u>forlorn</u>.
Jane was <u>forlorn</u> when all her friends went home.
The deserted house looked <u>forlorn</u>.

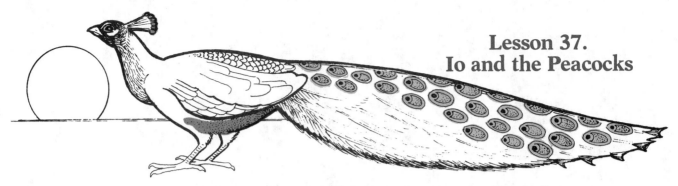

Zeus, the <u>reigning</u> <u>monarch</u> of the gods, once grew <u>fond</u> of an <u>attractive</u> <u>maiden</u> named Io. To escape the <u>curious</u> <u>gaze</u> of Hera, the <u>crafty</u> <u>sovereign</u> <u>concealed</u> himself behind a <u>huge</u> cloud. Hera, becoming <u>suspicious</u>, brushed the cloud aside to <u>reveal</u>—Zeus <u>caressing</u> a <u>handsome</u> white <u>heifer</u>! Zeus had <u>alertly</u> <u>transformed</u> the <u>charming</u> <u>damsel</u> into a cow, Hera's <u>favorite</u> animal.

"What a <u>handsome</u> <u>beast</u>," <u>exclaimed</u> Hera. "Surely, my lord, you will <u>grant</u> her to me, will you not?"

Zeus was <u>reluctant</u> to <u>abandon</u> Io, but he <u>hesitated</u> to act boldly. <u>Momentarily</u> <u>bewildered</u>, Zeus felt <u>compelled</u> to <u>grant</u> Hera her <u>request</u>. Hera then <u>bade</u> her trusted <u>sentry</u>, Argus, to stand over the <u>forlorn</u> <u>heifer</u>. Argus was a <u>huge</u> <u>creature</u> with no fewer than a hundred eyes. He needed to close only two in order to sleep, so he was the perfect <u>sentry</u>.

And so poor <u>captive</u> Io was <u>constantly</u> <u>spied</u> on by Argus, whose steady <u>gaze</u> never <u>faltered</u>. Even Zeus who wanted to <u>rescue</u> Io, was puzzled about how to do so. At last he <u>despatched</u> Hermes, the clever messenger of the gods, to <u>devise</u> a <u>scheme</u> to <u>destroy</u> Argus, or to <u>dispose</u> of him.

Hermes began by playing soft tunes on his flute. Argus' eyes began slowly to droop, but he <u>obstinately</u> refused to fall into deep <u>slumber</u>. Hermes then began to tell long, dull stories. One by one the <u>huge</u> <u>creature's</u> eyes closed. Hermes <u>leaped</u> <u>instantly</u> to his feet, <u>seized</u> his sword, and hacked off his head. Then he led the <u>heifer</u> to safety.

When Hera returned to see what was going on, she found the body. <u>Weeping</u> with <u>remorse</u>, the goddess gently removed Argus' eyes and fastened them to the flowing tail of her <u>favorite</u> <u>fowl</u>, the peacock.

And so, say the <u>ancient</u> Greek myths, when you see the proud peacocks <u>strutting</u> around, remember that those <u>brilliant</u> blue spots on the birds' feathers are the eyes of Argus, Hera's <u>loyal</u> <u>sentry</u>.

Lesson 38
Vocabulary

1. **bestow** _____ / bi stō / v.
   synonyms: give, present / pri zent' /
   A rich person bestowed a million dollars on our public library.
   Much honor was bestowed on the brave hero.

---

2. **credit** _____ / kred' it / n., v.
   I give you credit for doing a good job. (n.)
   A person who pays his bills has good credit. (n.)
   That fine child is a credit to the school. (n.)
   The coach credited Paul with winning the game. (v.)
   The bank credited my account with twenty dollars. (v.)
   noun: creditor
   adjective: creditable

---

3. **artistic** _____ / är tis' tik / adj.
   That's an artistic arrangement of flowers.
   There are many artistic children in the school.
   nouns: art, artist

---

4. **tapestry** _____ / tap' is trē / n.
   We still have tapestries woven more than 600 years ago.
   Our couch is covered with tapestry, but it is a new piece of cloth.

---

5. **fame** _____ / fām / n.
synonym: reputation
The explorer's <u>fame</u> spread far and wide.
adjectives: famous, famed

6. **arrogant** _____ / ar′ ə gənt / adj.
synonyms: haughty, proud
antonym: humble
That <u>arrogant</u> person thinks no one is as good as she.
noun: arrogance

7. **evident** _____ / ev′ ə dənt / adj.
synonyms: obvious, plain, clear
Your report makes it <u>evident</u> that you liked the book.
noun: evidence

8. **space** _____ / spās / n., v.
There is <u>space</u> for 50 people on the bus. (n.)
Astronauts have gone into outer <u>space</u>. (n.)
Leave a <u>space</u> between each word in a written sentence. (n.)
<u>Space</u> your words carefully. (v.)

9. **publicly** _____ / pub′ lik lē / adv.
synonym: openly
antonym: privately
We sang <u>publicly</u> for the first time.
Charles admitted his mistake <u>publicly</u>.
adjective: public

10. **loom** _____ / lüm / n.
A <u>loom</u> is a machine for weaving cloth.
homograph: loom / lüm / v. (appear suddenly)
An iceberg <u>loomed</u> ahead of the ship.

Lesson 38.
Arachne
and the Spider

The goddess Athena <u>bestowed</u> her name to the city of Athens, and she is given <u>credit</u> for giving the olive tree to the <u>ancient</u> Greeks. Of all the goddesses, she was the most skillful at <u>artistic</u> weaving and needlework.

There once lived an <u>attractive</u> Greek <u>maiden</u> named Arachne, who became quite clever at weaving <u>delicate</u> tapestries. Her friends' <u>flattery</u> soon turned her head. As her <u>fame</u> grew, the once <u>modest</u> girl became <u>haughty</u> and <u>arrogant</u>. She <u>boasted</u> <u>constantly</u> about her <u>ability</u> and <u>declared</u> that her <u>talent</u> was <u>superior</u> to that of Athena.

"I have never <u>inspected</u> Athena's woven <u>creations</u>," she <u>sneered</u>, "but it is quite <u>evident</u> that mine are <u>superior</u> to hers. I would not <u>hesitate</u> to enter a contest to <u>determine</u> who is the more <u>talented</u>."

<u>Noble</u> Athena was <u>reluctant</u> to <u>quarrel</u> <u>publicly</u> with a <u>mortal</u>, but the gods <u>urged</u> her to <u>respond</u> to Arachne's <u>scornful</u> <u>challenge</u>. The contest was therefore arranged. It was to be held in the <u>presence</u> of the gods, and a <u>host</u> of <u>loyal</u> <u>spectators</u> <u>assembled</u> to give <u>vocal</u> <u>support</u> to their <u>favorite</u>.

The <u>looms</u> were set up, and amid loud <u>applause</u> the <u>signal</u> to begin was sounded. Arachne did her very best to <u>achieve</u> a <u>triumph</u> over the goddess, but she was no match for her <u>rival</u>. The <u>spectators</u> <u>gasped</u> in <u>astonishment</u> at Athena's <u>brilliant</u> <u>display</u> of skill. Arachne began to <u>falter</u> and was finally <u>obliged</u> to <u>yield</u>. <u>Weeping</u> <u>remorsefully</u>, the <u>impulsive</u> <u>maiden</u> <u>resolved</u> to <u>fling</u> herself from the mountain <u>summit</u> to the sharp rocks below. At the very <u>moment</u> that she <u>plunged</u> into <u>space</u>, Athena <u>alertly</u> <u>transformed</u> her into—a spider!

And so, when you see a spider skillfully weaving her web, be reminded that she is Arachne, the <u>mortal</u> <u>maiden</u> who <u>defied</u> Athena and foolishly <u>challenged</u> one of the gods.

Lesson 39
Vocabulary

1. **fabulous** _____ / fab′ yə ləs / adj.
   synonyms: unbelievable, wonderful
   The moon landing was a fabulous achievement.
   The family had a fabulous vacation.
   Paul Bunyan stories are fabulous tales.
   noun: fable

---

2. **glisten** _____ / glis′ ən / n., v.
   synonyms: sparkle, shine, glitter, gleam
   The jewels in her ring glistened. (v.)
   The children's eyes glistened when they saw the lighted Christmas
   tree. (v.)
   The floor has a glisten after it has been polished. (n.)
   Ice on the trees has the glisten of diamonds. (n.)

---

3. **marvelous** _____ / mär′ və ləs / adj.
   synonyms: fabulous, wonderful
   We had a marvelous time at the picnic.
   Television is a marvelous invention.
   noun: marvel

---

4. **military** _____ / mil′ ə ter′ ē / n., adj.
   The band played military music. (adj.)
   West Point is a military college. (adj.)
   Jake decided to join the military. (n.)
   adjective: militant

---

5. **devoted** _____ / di vōt′ əd / adj.
   synonyms: loyal, faithful
   A dog is a devoted companion.
   Ruth and I are devoted friends.
   noun: devotion
   verb: devote

---

6. **sentinel** _____ / sen′ tə nəl / n.
   synonyms: sentry, guard, watchman
   The <u>sentinel</u> stood guard all night.

7. **perceive** _____ / pər sēv′ / v.
   synonyms: see, understand, realize
   I <u>perceive</u> that you are puzzled.
   Do you <u>perceive</u> that bird in the bush?
   noun: perception
   adjective: perceptible

8. **betray** _____ / bi tra′ / v.
   The traitor <u>betrayed</u> his country.
   "Don't <u>betray</u> my secret," pleaded Sally.
   noun: betrayal

9. **flexible** _____ / flek′ sə bəl / adj.
   synonym: bendable
   antonyms: unbendable, stiff, inflexible
   A <u>flexible</u> tube can be bent to go around objects.
   Jane is <u>flexible</u> and willing to change her plans.
   verb: flex

10. **expose** _____ / ek spōz′ / v.
    synonyms: uncover, show, display
    antonyms: conceal, hide
    The crime was <u>exposed</u> by good police work.
    Shopkeepers must <u>expose</u> their goods.
    Firemen are often <u>exposed</u> to danger.
    nouns: exposure, exposition

Lesson 39.
Mars and the Rooster

Aphrodite, known as Venus to the Romans, was the goddess of love and beauty. Oddly enough, this most beautiful of all the goddesses was wed to Vulcan, the lame, ugly god who was a fabulous worker in metal products. Vulcan toiled day and night in his gloomy underground workshop. There he produced glistening jewelry and marvelous armor and other military weapons.

The charming but fickle Venus gradually grew weary of ugly, dirty Vulcan. All of the other gods were in love with Venus and hoped that she might someday dispose of her husband and marry one of them.

Arrogant Ares, whom the Romans knew as Mars, was the handsome god of war. He and Venus grew fond of each other. It was rumored that they frequently met while Vulcan was occupied with his chores. They might chatter and gossip merrily the whole night long. Mars would bring with him his devoted companion, Alectryon. He bade him serve as a sentinel for him and Venus.

"Be alert," he exclaimed sternly. "When you perceive the first rays of dawn, signal to us. Apollo thoroughly despises me. If he should see me with Venus, he will promptly reveal our secret and expose us to public ridicule."

"Fear not, my lord," declared Alectryon. "You may rely on me. I shall be your vigilant sentry."

But Alectryon, who was utterly exhausted, promptly fell asleep. As Mars had suspected, Apollo lost no time in betraying the two. The indignant husband, Vulcan, flung a flexible metal net over them. Struggle as they would, the captives could not free themselves. Vulcan then summoned the other gods, who roared with laughter at the guilty pair. When Vulcan reluctantly freed him, Mars gave Alectryon a severe beating and transformed his former friend into—a rooster!

Now, say the myths, when you hear a rooster crow shrilly at dawn, remember that it is Alectryon belatedly warning the whole world that Apollo is approaching in his chariot.

Lesson 40
Vocabulary

1. **mysterious** _____ / mi stir' ē əs / adj.
   synonyms: hidden, secret, puzzling, odd
   Mysterious noise came from the woods.
   The note was written in a mysterious code.
   Electricity is mysterious to me.
   noun: mystery
   verb: mystify

___

2. **grace** _____ / grās / n.
   He says grace before meals.
   A true lady has grace and charm.
   A good dancer has grace.
   The king showed grace to his enemies.
   adjectives: graceful, ungraceful

___

3. **toyed** _____ / toid / v.
   The cat toyed with the mouse.
   noun: toy

___

4. **repress** _____ / re pres' / v.
   Joan tried to repress her cough.
   Ted tried to repress his fear.
   noun: repression
   adjective: repressive

___

5. **flutter** _____ / flut' ər / n., v.
   synonyms: wave, tremble (v.),
           trembling, shaking (n.)
   The flag fluttered in the breeze. (v.)
   Baby birds fluttered near the nest. (v.)
   I like to see the flutter of leaves. (n.)
   Jenny felt a flutter when she began to sing. (n.)

___

6. **afflict** _____ / ə flikt′ / v.
   synonyms: trouble, disturb
   Hardships <u>afflicted</u> the pioneers.
   Helen Keller was <u>afflicted</u> with blindness and deafness.
   noun: affliction

7. **score** _____ / skôr / n., v.
   The <u>score</u> in the game is tied. (n.)
   He made a perfect test <u>score</u>. (n.)
   <u>Scores</u> of people attended the show. (n.)
   A <u>score</u> of books is twenty books. (n.)
   We <u>scored</u> three runs to win the game. (v.)
   The children <u>scored</u> their own tests. (v.)

8. **sustain** _____ / sə stān′ / v.
   synonyms: support, aid, uphold
   Steel beams <u>sustain</u> this building.
   Food <u>sustains</u> your body.
   Hope <u>sustained</u> the parents of the sick boy.
   noun: sustenance

9. **prejudice** _____ / prej′ ə dis / n., v.
   A <u>prejudice</u> is an unfair opinion. (n.)
   Don't let one bad experience <u>prejudice</u> you against something. (v.)
   adjective: prejudiced

10. **Titan** _____ / tī tən / n.
    synonym: giant
    Atlas was a <u>Titan</u> in the Greek myths.
    related noun: titan (powerful businessman)
    adjective: titanic

Lesson 40.
The Pandora's Box

Zeus once wished to punish the men on earth for having accepted the gift of fire, which had at first been used by only gods. The gods, say the ancient myths, craftily resolved to create women to annoy the men and make their lives miserable.

Each god and goddess helped to make the first female fabulously attractive. One god bestowed beauty upon her. Another gave her grace and modesty. Still another gave her feminine charm. Another gave her marvelous music ability and artistic talent. They named her Pandora, which means "the gift of all the gods." They then gave her a mysterious box.

"Take the box," they bade her solemnly, "but beware! You must never, never venture to open it."

Pandora was offered as a wife to Epimetheus, a huge Titan who was not very bright. He was delighted and became an adoring and devoted husband. It did not take long for him to perceive that his bride had one serious fault: she was curious, hopelessly curious. She apparently felt compelled to stick her pretty nose into everything. Of course, she could hardly resist the box the gods had despatched with her. Daily she toyed with the lid and dreamed of the treasures the box might reveal. At last she was unable to repress her curiosity any longer. She hesitated only a moment longer. Impulsively she flung the lid open and peered eagerly inside.

To her dismay, out fluttered a host of ugly little moths. They flew out of an open window and soared away. The gods had hidden in the creatures' bodies all the evils that afflict mankind. Out of the box emerged poverty, vanity, envy, famine, pain, prejudice, and scores of others. With a shriek of terror, the poor maiden slammed the lid. Forlorn Pandora gazed remorsefully at the box and burst into tears. At last she cautiously raised the lid again. To her amazement, one tiny winged creature emerged. It was—hope! One of the gods had slyly slipped hope into Pandora's box. And so, say the myths, although mortals must suffer, they will always have hope to sustain them.

Lesson 41
Vocabulary

1. **widower** _____ / wid′ ō ər / n.
   antonym: widow
   Uncle Paul became a <u>widower</u> when his wife died.

---

2. **considerate** _____ / kən sid′ ə rət / adj.
   synonym: thoughtful
   antonym: inconsiderate
   Helping a new pupil is <u>considerate</u>.
   noun: consideration
   verb: consider

---

3. **cinders** _____ / sin′ dərz / n.
   A lot of <u>cinders</u> were left in the fireplace.

---

4. **protest** _____ / prə test′ / v.,
   / prō′ test / n.
   synonyms: object / əb jekt′ / (v.), objection (n.)
   People often <u>protest</u> new taxes. (v.)
   The fans made a noisy <u>protest</u> when the batter was called out. (n.)

---

5. **abuse** _____ / ə būz′ / v.,
   / ə būs′ / n.
   synonyms: misuse (v.), cruelty (n.)
   The poor dog was <u>abused</u> by its master. (v.)
   <u>Abuse</u> made the dog fear people. (n.)
   adjective: abusive

---

6. **series** _____ / sir' ēz / n.
   The alphabet is a <u>series</u> of letters.
   We've had a <u>series</u> of rainy days lately.
   The Nancy Drew books were a <u>series</u> of mysteries.
   noun: serial

7. **ball** _____ / bôl / n.
   synonym: party
   The <u>ball</u> lasted far past midnight.
   homograph: ball (round object)

8. **humble** _____ / hum' bəl / v., adj.
   synonym: modest, lowly (adj.)
   antonyms: haughty, proud, conceited (adj.)
   She is <u>humble</u> about her talents. (adj.)
   Lincoln came from a <u>humble</u> home. (adj.)
   He is willing to accept a <u>humble</u> job. (adj.)
   Losing a game can <u>humble</u> a proud team. (v.)
   noun: humility

9. **coach** _____ / kōch / n., v.
   The king rode in a fine <u>coach</u>. (n.)
   The railroad train has three <u>coaches</u>. (n.)
   Mr. Lane is the football <u>coach</u>. (n.)
   Mr. Lane <u>coaches</u> the team. (v.)

10. **stammer** _____ / stam' ər / n., v.
    synonym: stutter
    He <u>stammered</u> nervously when he spoke. (v.)
    Some people have a nervous <u>stammer</u>. (n.)

Lesson 41.
Cinderella, Part 1

There once was a <u>widower</u> who decided to <u>wed</u> a second time. His new wife turned out to be mean and selfish. She had two rather ugly daughters who were as unpleasant as the mother. The <u>widower</u> also had a daughter, a <u>modest</u>, <u>attractive</u> <u>damsel</u>. She was as kind and <u>considerate</u> as her stepsisters were cruel and spiteful.

The stepmother soon became <u>envious</u> of her new step-daughter because she was more <u>charming</u> and <u>graceful</u> than her own <u>quarrelsome</u> girls. She therefore <u>compelled</u> her step-daughter to do all the dirty household <u>chores</u> and to sit in the ashes and <u>cinders</u> in the fireplace when she was through. The cruel stepsisters therefore began to call her Cinderella.

Cinderella <u>hesitated</u> to complain to her father, for he was too <u>timid</u> to <u>protest</u> the <u>abuse</u> with which she was <u>afflicted</u>.

It happened that the king's son <u>declared</u> <u>publicly</u> that he would be <u>host</u> at a <u>series</u> of <u>balls</u> at the <u>monarch's</u> palace. Like many other <u>prosperous</u> and <u>wealthy</u> young ladies, the two stepsisters were <u>delighted</u> to receive invitations. They <u>chattered</u> endlessly about the <u>elegant</u> gowns they would wear and if the <u>handsome</u> young <u>sovereign</u> might fall in love with one of them and <u>propose</u> to her. Cinderella was <u>obliged</u> to polish their <u>glistening</u> jewels and curl their hair for them.

"Don't you wish you could go to the <u>ball</u>?" <u>jeered</u> one of the <u>haughty</u> sisters.

"Oh, yes," exclaimed Cinderella, "but a <u>humble</u> <u>creature</u> like me cannot dream of attending the prince's <u>splendid</u> <u>affair</u>."

"You are right, Cinderella. The <u>wealthy</u> and <u>noble</u> <u>spectators</u> would <u>ridicule</u> you," said the stepsister with a <u>superior</u> smile.

At last the night of the first splendid ball arrived. Poor Cinderella saw her two stepsisters and her stepmother depart in a fine coach drawn by four noble steeds. She could not repress a few tears as she returned to her fireplace.

Suddenly she was startled by a light footstep. To her amazement, she became aware of the presence of a tiny fairy mutely gazing at her.

"Who—who are you?" she stammered.

"I'm your fairy godmother," retorted the mysterious stranger. "I'm here to help you. You want to go to the ball, don't you?"

Lesson 42
Vocabulary

1. **fetch** _____ / fech / v.
   synonyms: bring, sell (for)
   antonym: send
   Spot <u>fetches</u> the ball when I throw it.
   Please <u>fetch</u> my slippers.
   What are eggs <u>fetching</u> at the store?

2. **wand** _____ / wond / n.
   synonyms: stick, rod
   The fairy godmother held a magic <u>wand</u>.

3. **shabby** _____ / shab′ ē / adj.
   synonyms: ragged, tattered, run down, mean
   Her old coat looks <u>shabby</u>.
   We fixed our <u>shabby</u> fence.
   This sweater is <u>shabbier</u> than that one.
   That is the <u>shabbiest</u> yard on the block.
   Neglecting your friends is <u>shabby</u>.

4. **garment** _____ / gär′ mənt / n.
   The beggar's <u>garments</u> were shabby.
   It's time to wear winter <u>garments</u>.

5. **chuckle** _____ / chuk′ əl / n., v.
   synonym: laugh
   I <u>chuckle</u> when I read the comics. (v.)
   The joke gave me a <u>chuckle</u>. (n.)

6. **magnificent** _____ / mag ni' fə sənt / adj.
   synonyms: grand, beautiful, fine
   The Grand Canyon is a <u>magnificent</u> sight.
   The Capitol in Washington is <u>magnificent</u>.
   noun: magnificence

7. **identity** _____ / ī den' tə tē / n.
   The police know the robber's <u>identity</u>.
   I guessed your <u>identity</u> by your voice.
   verb: identify
   related noun: identification

8. **courteous** _____ / kėr' tē əs / adj.
   synonyms: mannerly, considerate
   antonyms: discourteous, rude
   <u>Courteous</u> people wait their turns in line.
   <u>Discourteous</u> people push ahead of others.
   noun: courtesy

9. **soil** _____ / soil / v.
   Don't <u>soil</u> your clean shirt.
   adjective: soiled
   homograph: soil (earth, ground)

10. **gallant** _____ / gal' ənt / adj.
    synonyms: noble, brave
    King Arthur's knights were <u>gallant</u> men.
    The troops fought a <u>gallant</u> battle.
    noun: gallantry
    adverb: gallantly

Lesson 42.
Cinderella, Part 2

"Oh yes, I should be <u>delighted</u> to go to the prince's <u>ball</u>," <u>gasped</u> Cinderella. "Anybody would."

"Then <u>trot</u> out to the garden and <u>fetch</u> me the biggest pumpkin you can find."

Cinderella returned a few <u>moments</u> later, <u>clutching</u> a <u>huge</u> pumpkin in her <u>slender</u> arms. The godmother struck the pumpkin with her magic <u>wand</u>. <u>Instantly</u> it became a <u>splendid</u> golden <u>coach</u>.

"Now <u>fetch</u> me those mousetrap cages from the pantry."

Cinderella brought them in. The wire cages held six <u>plump</u> mice <u>securely</u> <u>captive</u>. As each mouse <u>attempted</u> to <u>scamper</u> away, she struck it with her magic <u>wand</u> and <u>transformed</u> it into a <u>handsome</u> black <u>steed</u>.

"Are you ready, Cinderella?" asked the godmother.

"I can't go in these <u>shabby</u> <u>garments</u>," <u>protested</u> Cinderella. Her godmother <u>chuckled</u> <u>merrily</u> and tapped her with her <u>marvelous</u> <u>wand</u>.

<u>Instantly</u> Cinderella's <u>soiled</u> rags became a beautiful silk gown, and on her feet their appeared a pair of <u>dainty</u> glass slippers.

"Now go, my dear," said the godmother, "but remember! That magic ends at twelve o'clock. If you <u>linger</u> one <u>instant</u> after midnight, the <u>coach</u>, the horses, and your <u>elegant</u> <u>garments</u> will disappear."

When Cinderella arrived at the <u>magnificent</u> <u>royal</u> palace, the prince <u>gasped</u> at her beauty. He <u>gallantly</u> <u>supported</u> her as she <u>timidly</u> <u>descended</u> from her <u>coach</u>. He <u>seized</u> her <u>delicate</u> hand and led her past the <u>assembled</u> <u>guests</u>, who <u>stared</u> at her in <u>astonishment</u>.

The prince was <u>evidently</u> so <u>charmed</u> by Cinderella that he danced only with her instead of <u>mingling</u> with his <u>guests</u>. The stepmother and her daughters never <u>suspected</u> the <u>identity</u> of the prince's <u>favorite</u> dancing <u>companion</u>. When the clock struck fifteen minutes before twelve, Cinderella <u>courteously</u> <u>bade</u> the prince farewell. She got back home in the nick of time.

Lesson 43
Vocabulary

1. **assure** _____ / ə shŭr / v.
   They <u>assured</u> us the bridge was safe.
   noun: assurance
   adverb: assuredly

---

2. **similar** _____ / sim′ ə lər / adj.
   Synonyms have <u>similar</u> meanings.
   A brook and a creek are <u>similar.</u>
   noun: similarity

---

3. **frantic** _____ / fran′ tik / adj.
   synonym: excited
   There was a <u>frantic</u> search for gold in 1849.
   We were <u>frantic</u> when the little girl was lost.
   The dog made a <u>frantic</u> attempt to catch the rabbit.
   adverb: frantically

---

4. **haste** _____ / hāst / n.
   synonym: hurry
   In her <u>haste</u>, Rose dropped her books.
   verb: hasten / hās′ ən /
   adverb: hastily

---

5. **hobble** _____ / hob′ əl / n., v.
synonym: limp (v.)
Pete <u>hobbles</u> off the football field. (v.)
The cowboy <u>hobbled</u> his horse for the night. (v.)
Pete walked with a <u>hobble</u>. (n.)

6. **mourn** _____ / môrn / v.
synonym: grieve
The nation <u>mourned</u> the death of the President.
noun: mourning
adjective: mournful
homonym: morn (the first part of the day)

7. **realm** _____ / relm / n.
synonyms: kingdom, region
Citizens obey the laws of the <u>realm</u>.
Bob is interested in the <u>realm</u> of science.

8. **uproar** _____ / up′ rôr / n.
synonyms: commotion, disturbance, hubbub
The angry workers were in an <u>uproar</u>.
adjective: uproarious

9. **cottage** _____ / kot′ ij / n.
synonyms: house, hut
She lives in a pretty little <u>cottage</u>.

10. **gale** _____ / gāl / n.
synonym: windstorm
The ship was tossed about in the <u>gale</u>.
A <u>gale</u> of laughter came from the auditorium.

Lesson 43.
Cinderella, Part 3

The whole kingdom buzzed with gossip and rumors about the mysterious maiden who had so utterly charmed the prince at the first ball. Many spectators flocked to the palace to see whether she would appear on the second night.

She did. Cinderella could hardly wait to go.

"Remember, my dear," warned her fairy godmother. "If you're not back by midnight—"

"I know, Godmother," cried Cinderella. "I assure you I'll not linger too long."

The second ball was similar to the first. The prince again devoted his time to Cinderella. The hours flew by. Suddenly Cinderella became aware that the huge palace clock was striking twelve! Frantic with fear, she raced for her golden coach. In her haste she lost one of her dainty glass slippers. Desperately clutching the other one, she realized that her elegant coach had disappeared. Her pretty silk gown, too, had again become the soiled old garment she worked in.

The bewildered prince had alertly pursued Cinderella when she fled in panic. He encountered only a shabbily dressed maiden hobbling down the street. He picked up her glass slipper and stared mournfully at it.

The whole realm was in an uproar the next day. The prince, determined to marry Cinderella, despatched his servants to find her. From house to house, they trudged with the glass slipper. Every young lady was obliged to try it on. The prince proclaimed publicly that he would marry the one whom the slipper fit.

The daughters of the <u>noble</u> and <u>wealthy</u> families tried to squeeze their feet into the glass slipper. The servants came at last to Cinderella's <u>humble</u> <u>cottage</u>. The stepsisters also tried <u>desperately</u> but <u>vainly</u> to force their big feet into the slipper.

"May I try it on?" asked Cinderella <u>timidly</u>.

"You?" cried the stepsisters <u>scornfully</u>. They and their mother burst into <u>gales</u> of laughter.

Of course the slipper fit perfectly, and Cinderella <u>calmly</u> <u>produced</u> the missing slipper. The prince was <u>delighted</u>. He <u>proposed</u> and was <u>accepted</u> <u>instantly</u>. The prince and Cinderella were <u>promptly</u> married and lived happily ever after.

Lesson 44
Mastery Test

The Vocabulary Booster lesson for today is your Mastery Test for Lessons 34–43.

☐ Prepare for the Mastery Test by reviewing your notebook pages for Lessons 34–43.

☐ Your teacher will distribute the test. Underline the word or phrase that gives the best definition of the test word. The first one is done for you.

EXAMPLE:

1. **vigil** a) sleepiness b) something that you fear c) illness d) <u>a long watch</u>

☐ Review the test with your teacher and class.

☐ Record your Mastery Test score on the Mastery Test Progress Chart at the back of the book.

Lesson 45
Vocabulary

1. **elderly** _____ / el' dər lē / adj.
   synonym: old
   antonym: young
   Grandpa is <u>elderly</u> but full of pep.
   noun: elder
   adjectives: elder, eldest

---

2. **career** _____ / kə rir' / n.
   synonyms: work, profession
   She plans to make politics her <u>career</u>.

---

3. **grim** _____ / grim / adj.
   synonyms: harsh, stern, serious
   Father looked <u>grim</u> when he heard about the broken window.
   Some ghost stories are too <u>grim</u> for little children.

---

4. **mood** _____ / müd / n.
   Everyone at the party was in a cheerful <u>mood</u>.
   adjective: moody

---

5. **snarl** _____ / snärl / n., v.
   synonym: growl
   The dogs <u>snarled</u> at the stranger. (v.)
   "Get off my property," <u>snarled</u> the man. (v.)
   The bully <u>snarled</u> threats at the small children. (v.)
   homograph: snarl (tangle)
   Don't <u>snarl</u> your thread. (v.)
   The traffic is in a <u>snarl</u>. (n.)

---

6. **bass** _____ / bās / n., adj.
   Joe has a deep <u>bass</u> voice. (adj.)
   Joe and Paul are both <u>basses</u>. (n.)
   homonym: base / bās / n., v.
           The runner reached second <u>base</u>. (n.)
           There is rock at the <u>base</u> of the hill. (n.)
           Your grade is <u>based</u> on your test score. (v.)
   [Watch out for bass / bas /, a fish.]

7. **gratitude** _____ / grat′ ə tüd / n.
   synonym: thankfulness
   antonym: ingratitude
   We show <u>gratitude</u> to those who help us.
   adjective: grateful

8. **comrade** _____ / kom′ rad / n.
   synonyms: friend, companion
   Dan and his <u>comrades</u> went fishing.
   adjective: comradely
   related noun: comradeship

9. **dense** _____ / dens / adj.
   synonyms: thick, close (together)
   There was <u>dense</u> fog this morning.
   There was a <u>dense</u> crowd at the game.
   It is dark in a <u>dense</u> forest.
   noun: density

10. **presently** _____ / prez′ ənt lē / adv.
    synonym: soon, now
    I'll see you <u>presently</u>.
    Kim is <u>presently</u> at her aunt's.
    adjective: present / prez′ ənt /

Lesson 45.
The Bremen Musicians, Part I

An <u>elderly</u> donkey, <u>suspecting</u> that his owner was about to get rid of him, <u>resolved</u> to begin a new <u>career</u> as a musician in Bremen town. On his way he <u>spied</u> an old dog lying in the shade of a tree. The dog was <u>evidently</u> in a <u>grim</u> <u>mood</u>, so the donkey <u>paused</u> to ask what ailed him.

"After years of <u>loyal</u> and <u>devoted</u> <u>service</u>, I am about to be <u>tossed</u> out of house and home," he <u>snarled</u>.

"Why not join me?" <u>urged</u> the donkey. "I'm on my way to see Bremen to <u>seek</u> my <u>fortune</u> as a musician. You have a <u>splendid</u> <u>bass</u> voice."

"I'm with you," <u>exclaimed</u> the dog.

Together the two <u>trotted</u> down the road to Bremen. Before long they <u>encountered</u> an old cat <u>mournfully</u> <u>gnawing</u> on a piece of cheese. In <u>response</u> to the donkey's question, she cried <u>indignantly</u>, "My owner <u>threatens</u> to <u>dispose</u> of me because I can no longer <u>scamper</u> about <u>vigorously</u> and <u>pounce</u> on the rats that <u>infest</u> his house. Such <u>gratitude</u>!"

"We're off to become musicians in Bremen," said the donkey. "You have a <u>magnificent</u> voice, Cat. Why not join us?"

The old cat did so. Soon the three <u>companions</u> passed an old rooster who was crowing <u>furiously</u>.

"And what may be the matter?" asked the donkey <u>courteously</u>.

"My owner is having <u>guests</u> in tomorrow and is <u>scheming</u> to make soup of me," <u>wailed</u> the rooster.

"We're on the way to Bremen to become musicians," said the donkey <u>sympathetically</u>. "You're welcome to come along. You'd make a <u>talented</u> musician, I'm sure."

"Gladly," said the <u>flattered</u> old rooster, springing <u>instantly</u> onto the donkey's back.

The four new comrades had to spend the night in a dense, gloomy forest. The donkey and the dog lay down under a huge tree. The cat clambered up into the swaying branches. The rooster fluttered up to an upper limb and stared curiously around as he balanced himself.

"I see a light glistening in the distance," he called down to his friends. "Perhaps we can find a dwelling place superior by far to this tree."

"That's odd," murmured the donkey. "I propose that we venture onward and inspect the place." The others agreed, and the four were presently on their way to the mysterious light.

Lesson 46
Vocabulary

1. **band** _____ / band / n., v.
   synonym: group (n.)
   A band led the parade down the street. (n.)
   A band of pupils raked the schoolyard. (n.)
   The girls banded together to make posters. (v.)

___

2. **scramble** _____ / skram′ bəl / n., v.
   synonym: struggle
   The hikers scrambled up the hill. (v.)
   There was a scramble for the football. (n.)
   adjective: scrambled (mixed up)

___

3. **perch** _____ / pėrch / n., v.
   That branch is a fine perch for birds. (n.)
   We watched the game from our perch in the bleachers. (n.)
   Owls perch in trees. (v.)
   I perched on a stool and ate my lunch. (v.)
   homograph: perch (small fish)

___

4. **bray** _____ / brā / n., v.
   The donkey made a loud bray. (n.)
   Cows moo, horses neigh, and donkeys bray. (v.)

___

5. **shatter** _____ / shat′ ər / v.
   synonyms: break, splinter
   A rock <u>shattered</u> the window.
   Hope for a picnic was <u>shattered</u> by the rain.
   Nerves can be <u>shattered</u> by worries.
   adjective: shatterproof

6. **investigate** _____ / in ves′ tə gāt / v.
   synonym: examine
   Detectives <u>investigated</u> the crime.
   nouns: investigator, investigation

7. **grope** _____ / grōp / v.
   I <u>groped</u> in the dark for a flashlight.
   The blind man <u>groped</u> his way to the door.
   Nan <u>groped</u> for the right words to say.

8. **report** _____ / ri pôrt′ / n., v.
   synonym: account (n.)
   Newspapers <u>report</u> current events. (v.)
   We read sports <u>reports</u> in the paper. (n.)
   noun: reporter

9. **rascal** _____ / ras′ kəl / n.
   synonym: scoundrel
   <u>Rascals</u> stole the farmer's apples.
   My dog was a <u>rascal</u> when he was a puppy.

10. **villain** _____ / vil′ ən / n.
    synonyms: rascal, scoundrel
    That <u>villain</u> stole the widow's money.
    noun: villainy
    adjective: villainous

136

Lesson 46.
The Bremen Musicians, Part 2

The four comrades made their way cautiously through the dense, gloomy forest. Presently they came to a cottage. The donkey craned his neck and peered in a window.

"I see a table spread with fabulous fare," he whispered. "A band of robbers are in there making merry."

The four then set about devising a scheme to get the robbers out. The donkey put his forefeet on the window sill. The dog clambered up on his back. The cat scrambled up on the dog's shoulders. The rooster fluttered up and perched on the cat's head. The signal was given, and their music began. The donkey brayed. The dog barked, the cat shrieked, and the rooster crowed. Then they all plunged through the window, shattering the glass. The terrorized robbers scampered off in panic.

The four companions triumphantly devoured the food and sought out their resting places. The donkey lay down in the yard. The dog stretched out behind the door. The cat lay near the fireplace, and the rooster perched up on the roof.

Meanwhile the robbers decided that they had abandoned their former dwelling too soon. Perceiving that the cottage was dark, the robber leader despatched a volunteer to investigate. He crept into the kitchen and groped for a match to light a candle. The cat alertly leaped up and scratched his face. The robber darted outside the door where the startled dog instinctively bit him. As he crossed the yard, the donkey kicked him. The rooster, momentarily bewildered by the uproar, crowed shrilly.

The robber hobbled frantically back to report.

"A savage witch scratched my face," he stammered, "Then a big brute concealed behind the door stabbed me in the leg. Another enormous fellow holding vigil in the yard smashed me with a huge club, or some similar weapon. Meanwhile another old witch posted as a sentinel snarled, 'Kill the rascal! Kill the villain!' "

The robbers never dared return. The four musicians were so pleased with their new dwelling that they decided to spend the rest of their days there.

Lesson 47
Vocabulary

1. **gorgeous** _____ / gôr′ jəs / adj.
   synonyms: beautiful, magnificent, glorious, lovely
   antonyms: dull, ugly, plain, homely
   The lady wore a <u>gorgeous</u> gown.
   The sunset was <u>gorgeous</u>.

   _____

2. **emperor** _____ / em′ pər ər / n.
   An <u>emperor</u> is a powerful ruler.
   related nouns: empress, empire

   _____

3. **swindler** _____ / swind′ lər / n.
   A <u>swindler</u> sold her a fake diamond.
   noun and verb: swindle

   _____

4. **invisible** _____ / in viz′ ə bəl / adj.
   synonym: unseen
   antonym: visible
   Germs are <u>invisible</u> without a microscope.
   Your thoughts are <u>invisible</u>.
   nouns: invisibility, visibility

   _____

5. **official** _____ / ə fish′ əl / n., adj.
   The mayor is a city <u>official</u>. (n.)
   He has <u>official</u> duties. (adj.)
   related noun: office

   _____

6. **spectacles** _____ / spek′ tə kəlz / n.
   synonym: eyeglasses
   My <u>spectacles</u> help me see better.
   related noun: spectacle

7. **pattern** _____ / pat′ ərn / n.
   synonyms: model, guide
   Lou used a <u>pattern</u> when she made her dress.
   Billy is a <u>pattern</u> of good behavior.
   The wallpaper has a <u>pattern</u> of flowers.

8. **squander** _____ / skwan′ dər / v.
   synonym: waste
   The boy <u>squandered</u> his allowance on junk.
   Don't <u>squander</u> your time.

9. **fabric** _____ / fab′ rik / n.
   synonym: cloth
   The <u>fabric</u> in my coat is wool.
   Nylon is a man–made <u>fabric</u>.
   verb: fabricate
   related noun: fabrication

10. **dare** _____ / dãr / n., v.
    synonym: challenge
    Astronauts <u>dared</u> to explore outer space. (v.)
    Tim <u>dared</u> her to dive into the pool. (v.)
    Don't accept a foolish <u>dare</u>. (n.)
    adjective: daring

Lesson 47.
The Emperor's New Clothes

There once reigned an emperor who was so fond of new clothes that he squandered an enormous fortune to purchase them. One day two crafty swindlers appeared at the monarch's palace, pretending to be weavers.

"My comrade and I can weave the most gorgeous cloth you ever saw, I assure you," declared one of the shrewd villains. "The odd thing about our clothes is that they become invisible to stupid people and to officials who are unfit for their jobs."

The emperor was delighted to be enabled to identify stupid and unfit officials. He paid the rascals generously and urged them to proceed. They set up their looms, but constantly requested more and more money for silk and gold thread. The emperor despatched his top official to inspect the weaving.

The elderly official could see nothing at all on the looms.

"Goodness," he murmured, "can I be stupid? Am I unfit for my job? I dare not admit I can't see the stuff."

"It's fabulous!" he exclaimed, peering solemnly through his spectacles. "I've never seen any fabric to rival it."

The emperor sent a second official, who also stared—and saw nothing. He, too, praised the elegant cloth, the artistic patterns, and the brilliant colors.

Rumors about the marvelous cloth soon spread through the realm. The emperor resolved to investigate himself. He assembled a score of royal officials to observe the miraculous weavers at work.

"Isn't the cloth magnificent?" asked the two officials who had been deceived earlier. They pointed to the empty looms. Of course, the emperor saw nothing. The officials saw nothing, but all, including the sovereign, expressed their amazement at the talented swindlers' splendid feat. Everybody counseled the emperor to display his new garments publicly at the grand parade through the city streets.

For the parade the swindlers persuaded the emperor to strip down to his shorts. They pretended to help him get into his imaginary new garments. When he strutted proudly in the streets, everybody applauded.

"Marvelous! Handsome! Charming!" they cried. Of course nobody wanted to admit that the emperor had no new clothes on at all. At last a child cried out, "But he has nothing on!"

Presently the people began whispering to one another. At last they broke into roars of laughter.

"The emperor has nothing on at all!" they shouted.

The poor emperor knew they were right, but he proudly marched on—and on—and on.

Lesson 48
Vocabulary

1. **progress** ———————————— / prog′ rəs / n.

   / prə gres′ / v.

   You are making <u>progress</u> in school. (n.)
   The meeting is now in <u>progress</u>. (n.)
   We <u>progressed</u> along the highway. (v.)
   The planets <u>progress</u> around the sun. (v.)
   adjective: progressive
   related noun: progression

---

2. **comment** ———————————— / kom′ ənt / n., v.
   synonym: remark
   The teacher made some <u>comments</u> about my book report. (n.)
   "I like your work," she <u>commented</u>. (v.)
   related noun: commentator

---

3. **poultry** ———————————— / pōl′ trē / n.
   Most <u>poultry</u> farmers in the United States raise chickens.

---

4. **normal** ———————————— / nôr′ məl / adj.
   synonyms: usual, regular
   It's <u>normal</u> to laugh at a good joke.
   We'll follow our <u>normal</u> program today.
   adverb: normally

---

5. **tumble** ———————————— / tum′ bəl / n., v.
   synonym: fall
   The child <u>tumbled</u> out of bed. (v.)
   The wind <u>tumbled</u> a tree in our yard. (v.)
   The boy was not hurt in his <u>tumble</u>. (n.)
   related nouns: tumbler, tumbleweed
   adjective: tumble down

---

6. **frolic** _____ / frol′ ik / n., v.
   synonym: play
   Young animals <u>frolic</u> in the spring. (v.)
   The children <u>frolicked</u> in the yard. (v.)
   Most people enjoy an evening of fun and <u>frolic</u>. (n.)
   verb forms: frolic, frolicked, frolicking
   adjective: frolicsome

7. **hideous** _____ / hid′ ē əs / adj.
   synonyms: ugly, frightful
   antonyms: lovely, beautiful
   Some Halloween masks are <u>hideous</u>.
   Smallpox is a <u>hideous</u> disease.

8. **clumsy** _____ / klum′ zē / adj.
   synonym: awkward
   antonym: graceful
   The <u>clumsy</u> clown bumped into everything.
   We built a <u>clumsy</u> wagon out of a box.
   adjective forms: clumsier, clumsiest

9. **several** _____ / sev′ ər əl / adj.
   synonym: (a) few
   I've read <u>several</u> good books lately.
   <u>Several</u> children are absent.

10. **embarrass** _____ / em bar′ əs / v.
    Ruth was <u>embarrassed</u> when she spilled the milk.
    noun: embarrassment
    adjective: embarrassing
    [Watch out for the double letters in embarrass!]

Lesson 48.
The Ugly Duckling, Part 1

The mother duck sat on her nest hatching out her ducklings. Presently the egg shells began to crack and the ducklings came scrambling out—all, that is, but one.

"Making progress I see," commented the elderly duck who reigned sternly over the poultry yard.

"I've produced a superior brood," declared the mother proudly. "That last large egg hasn't cracked yet, I regret to say."

"Let me inspect that curious egg," quacked the elderly duck. "Ha! As I suspected! I assure you, my dear, that's a turkey egg. My counsel is to abandon it."

"No," said the mother obstinately as she resumed her place on the egg. "I'm determined to persist."

The large egg cracked at last. A great ugly duckling clumsily emerged from the shell. The mother duck gasped.

"Why, it's enormous!" she wailed. "Is it a turkey chick? I'll soon find out. I'll push him into the water. If he's a normal duckling, he'll swim instinctively."

One after the other, the mother duck tumbled her youngsters into the pond. The ducklings, including the big ugly fellow, were delighted and frolicked about vigorously in the water. The ugly one had not hesitated to plunge in. He swam quite gracefully and seemed to like water.

"He's certainly no turkey," chuckled the mother.

Pleased with her ducklings' performance, the mother led her family to the poultry yard. The ducks stared at the ugly duckling with ill-concealed contempt.

"Look at the odd fellow," exclaimed one "Get him out of here!" Several barnyard spectators glared at the embarrassed duckling.

A duck hastened over, struck him with her wing, and bit him.

"Let him alone!" protested the mother indignantly.

"He's hideous," sneered another haughty duck. "We don't want him to mingle with our children."

Poor Ugly Duckling became an object of ridicule and abuse in the poultry yard. The other ducks jeered at him and taunted him. The chickens and turkeys pursued him, pecked him, and bit him. Realizing that he could never overcome such violent prejudice, he resolved to flee. When no one was watching, he fluttered wearily over the fence and headed for the gloomy swamp where a colony of wild ducks were living.

Lesson 49
Vocabulary

1. **invade** _____ / in vād' / v.
   Enemy troops invaded the land.
   Grasshoppers invaded the field.
   nouns: invasion, invader

___

2. **sparkle** _____ / spär' kəl / n., v.
   synonyms: twinkle, shine, glitter
   A diamond ring sparkles. (v.)
   Jennie's eyes sparkled. (v.)
   I like dishes to have a sparkle. (n.)
   adjective: sparkling

___

3. **flap** _____ / flap / n., v.
   The wild geese flapped their wings. (v.)
   The shade flapped at the open window. (v.)
   Beavers make a flap on the water with their tails. (n.)
   Some coat pockets have flaps. (n.)

___

4. **temperate** _____ / tem' pər ət / adj.
   We usually have temperate weather in May.
   Temperate people don't lose their tempers.

___

5. **region** _____ / rē jən / n.
Oranges grow well in warm regions.
adjective: regional

6. **yearn** _____ / yern / v.
synonym: long (for)
The lonesome soldier yearned for home.
Jimmy yearned for a new bike.
noun: yearning

7. **arc** _____ / ärk / n.
synonym: curve, bend, arch
The rainbow forms an arc.
homonym: ark (Noah's boat)

8. **fragrant** _____ / frā′ grənt / adj.
synonym: sweet smelling
Roses are fragrant.
noun: fragrance

9. **bloom** _____ / blüm / n., v.
synonyms: blossom, flower
Flowers bloom in the spring. (v.)
There are many blooms on the plant. (n.)

10. **reject** _____ / ri jekt′ / v.
/ rē′ jekt / n.
synonym: refuse (v.)
castoff (n.)
He rejected my offer of help. (v.)
I put the rejects in the trash can (n.)
noun: rejection

Lesson 49.
The Ugly Duckling, Part 2

The Ugly Duckling barely escaped when a <u>band</u> of hunters <u>invaded</u> the swamp and shot down many of the wild ducks. He stayed there, <u>mournful</u> and <u>forlorn</u>, until fall.

One evening a <u>flock</u> of <u>handsome</u> swans <u>emerged</u> from behind some bushes. The Ugly Duckling <u>gasped</u>. He had never seen such <u>magnificent</u> <u>creatures</u>. They were a <u>sparkling</u> white in color, with long, <u>flexible</u> necks, <u>uttering</u> a strange cry as they <u>flapped</u> their <u>huge</u> wings and <u>soared</u> off to more <u>temperate</u> <u>regions</u>. The Ugly Duckling <u>yearned</u> <u>desperately</u> to join them, but he <u>realized</u> that he was still too <u>frail</u> for such a long <u>journey</u>.

A <u>generous</u> farmer took the Ugly Duckling in or he would never have <u>survived</u> the <u>severe</u> winter weather. At last spring returned, the Ugly Duckling discovered that he could fly. <u>Flapping</u> his wings vigorously, he <u>soared</u> high and far. <u>Spying</u> a beautiful garden, he <u>descended</u> in a long, <u>graceful</u> <u>arc</u>. Here the <u>dense</u> <u>vegetation</u> was already in <u>fragrant</u> <u>bloom</u>.

Suddenly he became <u>aware</u> of three <u>gorgeous</u> swans <u>approaching</u> <u>gracefully</u> on the pond. <u>Cautiously</u> the Ugly Duckling paddled toward them, fearing that they, like the <u>fowl</u> in the <u>poultry</u> yard, would <u>reject</u> him. As he drew near them, he <u>glanced</u> down at his <u>image</u> in the clear water. To his <u>astonishment</u>, he was no longer an ugly gray bird. Suddenly he <u>realized</u> that he was—a swan! Again and again he <u>gazed</u> happily at his <u>reflection</u>.

Several youngsters came racing toward the pond to feed their <u>favorite</u> pets, the swans.

"There is a new one!" <u>exclaimed</u> one of the children. "Now there are four <u>magnificent</u> swans!"

The <u>former</u> Ugly Duckling felt shy and <u>modestly</u> <u>thrust</u> his head under his wing. Remembering how he had once been <u>abused</u>, he <u>murmured</u> happily, "I am glad that I am now a <u>handsome</u> swan instead of an ugly duckling."

Lesson 50
Vocabulary

1. **swarm** _____ / swärm / n., v.
   synonym: group (n.)
   A swarm of children are at the swimming pool. (n.)
   Grasshoppers swarmed over the field. (v.)
   The fairgrounds swarmed with people. (v.)

_____

2. **effective** _____ / ə fek′ tiv / adj.
   antonym: ineffective
   This poster is an effective way to advertise the play.
   Yelling is an ineffective way to get what you want.
   noun: effect

_____

3. **council** _____ / koun′ səl / n.
   The student council talks over our school problems.
   homonym: counsel (advice or advise)

_____

4. **stroll** _____ / strōl / n., v.
   synonym: walk (slowly)
   Many people stroll through the park. (v.)
   A stroll in the park is very pleasant. (n.)

_____

5. **fee** _____ / fē / n.
   synonym: charge
   Our zoo has no entrance <u>fee</u>.

6. **guarantee** _____ / gar′ ən tē′ / n., v.
   synonyms: pledge, promise
   There is a three-year <u>guarantee</u> on my stove. (n.)
   I <u>guarantee</u> that I'll be there. (v.)

7. **guilder** _____ / gil′ dər / n.
   The miser buried his gold <u>guilders</u>.

8. **scowl** _____ / skoul / n., v.
   synonym: frown
   antonym: smile
   Mother <u>scowled</u> at the mischievous child. (v.)
   A <u>scowl</u> makes you look cross. (n.)

9. **bargain** _____ / bär′ gən / n., v.
   synonym: agreement, deal (n.)
   I made a <u>bargain</u> to cut the grass for five dollars. (n.)
   That dress is a <u>bargain</u> at such a low price. (n.)
   We <u>bargained</u> with the used car dealer. (v.)

10. **troop** _____ / trüp / n., v.
    synonym: group (n.)
    The captain led his <u>troop</u> of soldiers bravely. (n.)
    A lot of pupils <u>trooped</u> into the room. (v.)
    The young children <u>trooped</u> after the older ones. (v.)
    nouns: troops, trooper

Lesson 50.
The Pied Piper of Hamelin

Centuries ago, the German village of Hamelin was infested with rats—thousands of fierce, savage rats. They swarmed through the streets, invaded the houses, and embarrassed the Hamelin officials. They and the mayor had been unable to devise an effective scheme to get rid of the hideous pests. The elderly mayor, in a grim mood, summoned the city council to discuss their problem for the hundredth time.

As they sat scratching their heads, an odd-looking fellow strolled into their midst. He wore a long, shabby garment made of bright red and yellow fabric.

"I hear you are overrun with rats," he said. "Well, I've made a career of destroying rats. I'm a very superior rat catcher. I'm called Pied Piper, and I guarantee results. My fee is one thousand guilders."

"A thousand guilders?" exclaimed the mayor. "Make it fifty thousand! We'll be delighted to pay you your fee if you can only get rid of these hideous beasts."

The stranger produced a slender musical pipe and began to play a shrill tune. The rats came tumbling and scrambling out of the houses. Still playing he led them down to the river Weser. The Piper waded in, and the rats followed. Every last one was drowned.

The Piper returned to the city hall and <u>courteously</u> <u>re</u>quested his <u>fee</u> of a thousand <u>guilders</u>.

"You must be joking," bellowed the mayor, pretending to be <u>indignant</u>. "Surely you don't expect us to <u>squander</u> such a <u>huge</u> sum for disposing of a few rats! How about fifty <u>guilders</u>?"

The Pied Piper <u>scowled</u>.

"You made a promise," he said <u>calmly</u>. "I still have my pipe. Keep your <u>bargain</u> or I'll play a tune you won't like."

"Don't <u>threaten</u> me!" cried the mayor. "Go blow on your silly pipe."

The stranger <u>promptly</u> stepped into the street and began to play a <u>charming</u> tune. <u>Presently</u> the <u>village</u> children came <u>flocking</u> around him, unable to resist the <u>mysterious</u> music. Out of town he <u>trudged</u>, with the youngsters <u>trooping</u> <u>gleefully</u> after him. Up the neighboring mountain they <u>ascended</u>. Near the <u>summit</u> an opening appeared. The youngsters marched in time to the music like a <u>military</u> <u>troop</u>. They were never seen again.

It was <u>reported</u> years later that there lived in a nearby region a strange <u>colony</u> of people with the same names as the Hamelin children. They wear <u>curious</u> <u>garments</u> of red and yellow. Not one, it is said, ever breaks a promise.

Lesson 51
Vocabulary

1. **national** _____ / nash′ ə nəl / adj.
   synonym: nation-wide
   "The Star Spangled Banner" is our <u>national</u> anthem.
   There will be a <u>national</u> election in November.
   nouns: nation, nationality
   adverb: nationally

---

2. **legend** _____ / lej′ ənd / n.
   synonyms: story, folktale
   Have you read the Robin Hood <u>legends</u>?
   adjective: legendary

---

3. **native** _____ / na′ tiv / n., adj.
   Indians are <u>natives</u> of America. (n.)
   Corn is a <u>native</u> American plant. (adj.)

---

4. **appoint** _____ / ə point′ / v.
   The governor has <u>appointed</u> three judges.
   The time <u>appointed</u> for the meeting is six o'clock.
   nouns: appointment, appointee

---

5. **tyrant** _____ / tī′ rənt / n.
   The <u>tyrant</u> taxed the people cruelly.
   related noun: tyranny
   adjective: tyrannical

6. **patriot** _____ / pā′ trē ət / n.
   Paul Revere was an American <u>patriot</u>.
   related noun: patriotism
   adjective: patriotic

7. **erect** _____ / i rekt′ / v., adj.
   synonyms: build (v.), straight (adj.)
   We <u>erected</u> a flagpole in the front yard. (v.)
   The trees stood <u>erect</u> and tall. (adj.)

8. **salute** _____ / sə lüt′ / n., v.
   synonyms: honor, greet (v.), greeting (n.)
   We <u>saluted</u> the flag as it passed. (v.)
   The soldier stood erect and gave a <u>salute</u> by raising his hand to his forehead. (n.)

9. **pace** _____ / pās / n., v.
   synonym: step (n.), walk (v.)
   Al took four <u>paces</u> forward. (n.)
   He <u>walked</u> at a slow <u>pace</u>. (n.)
   Helen <u>paced</u> up and down the hall. (v.)

10. **growl** _____ / groul / n., v.
    "Get away. I'm busy," Sam <u>growled</u>. (v.)
    The angry dog <u>growled</u>. (v.)
    A dog's <u>growl</u> sounds frightening. (n.)

Lesson 51.
The Legend of William Tell

Centuries ago, gallant William Tell became a national Swiss hero, and his legend continues to live. During his time the Austrians invaded his tiny native land. The Austrian emperor was determined to reduce Switzerland to a helpless captive state. He appointed an arrogant tyrant named Gessler as his military official there.

To make the Swiss patriots realize that they had lost their freedom, Gessler hoisted Austrian military caps to the tops of tall poles he had erected in the Swiss public squares. He proclaimed that the Swiss people were to salute this symbol of Austrian might. Anybody who challenged, protested, or defied his order was to be instantly tossed into prison.

When Tell strolled by the pole in his native village with his seven-year-old son, he ignored the cap perched on the pole. The alert Austrian sentries promptly pounced upon him and his son, and dragged them before Gessler.

"I hear that you're a loyal Swiss patriot," snarled Gessler triumphantly. "I hear, too, that you've won fame for your talent as an archer. I'll show you how generous I can be. I'll grant you a chance to display your skill and gain your freedom."

Gessler summoned a soldier and bade him fetch an apple.

"Take the boy about a hundred paces down on the village square and put the apple on his head," he ordered.

Gessler then turned to Tell with a scowl.

"Now, noble patriot," he growled, "shoot the apple off the boy's head. If you succeed, I'll set you both free."

Glancing at the tyrant with visible contempt, Tell took two arrows from his quiver. Thrusting one into his shirt, he took aim with the other and shot the apple cleanly off the boy's head. Scores of loyal Swiss spectators who had flocked in the square to watch broke into applause.

Gessler was furious. He scowled at Tell.

"Quite a feat," he sneered. "You took two arrows from your quiver. You concealed the second one in your shirt. What was that second arrow meant for?"

"It was meant for your heart if I had as much grazed the boy's head, tyrant," retorted Tell calmly as he and the boy turned to go.

Lesson 52
Vocabulary

1. **predict** _____ / pri dikt′ / v.
   synonyms: foretell, forecast
   Rain is <u>predicted</u> for tomorrow.
   I <u>predict</u> that you'll do well on your test.
   noun: prediction

---

2. **rash** _____ / rash / adj.
   synonyms: hasty, reckless, careless
   antonyms: prudent, thoughtful
   He made a <u>rash</u> decision to quit his job.
   A <u>rash</u> person takes too many chances.
   homograph: rash (a breaking out on your skin)

---

3. **prudent** _____ / prü′ dənt / adj.
   synonym: wise
   antonym: rash
   It's <u>prudent</u> to get enough rest.
   A <u>prudent</u> person thinks ahead.
   noun: prudence

---

4. **heed** _____ / hēd / v., n.
   Beth tries to <u>heed</u> her grandmother's advice. (v.)
   The lifeguard took no <u>heed</u> for his own safety and rescued the child. (n.)
   Ruth gives a lot of <u>heed</u> to her studies. (n.)
   adjectives: heedful, heedless

---

5. **crave** _____ / krāv / v.
synonym: yearn (for), long (for)
I crave popcorn when I'm at the movies.
The puppy craved attention.
noun: craving

6. **covet** _____ / kuv′ ət / v.
synonym: desire
The woman coveted her sister's wealth.
adjective: covetous

7. **pout** _____ / pout / n., v.
Annie pouted when she didn't get her way. (v.)
The pout on her face makes her look very unpleasant. (n.)

8. **shrug** _____ / shrug / n., v.
She shrugged her shoulders with displeasure. (v.)
He answered her question with a shrug. (n.)

9. **liquid** _____ / lik′ wid / n.
Liquids can flow like water.
verb: liquefy

10. **grain** _____ / grān / n.
Wheat and oats are important grains.
I sprinkled a few grains of salt on my meat.
related noun: granary

Lesson 52.
The Golden Touch

Of course, anybody with <u>common</u> sense could have <u>predicted</u> what would happen. But King Midas was <u>evidently</u> a <u>rash</u> and not a <u>prudent</u> <u>monarch</u>. If he had only <u>heeded</u> the wine god's <u>counsel</u>—but then there would be no story.

King Midas was <u>greedy</u>. More than anything in the world he loved gold. He <u>craved</u> gold. He <u>coveted</u> gold. He was <u>wealthy</u>, but he <u>yearned</u> <u>constantly</u> for more to add to his <u>enormous</u> <u>fortune</u>.

Midas once did a favor for Bacchus, the Greek wine god. In <u>gratitude</u> Bacchus <u>generously</u> offered to <u>grant</u> him one wish. Midas' eyes <u>sparkled</u> with ill-<u>concealed</u> <u>greed</u>.

"I wish everything I touch would turn into gold," he cried <u>triumphantly</u>.

Bacchus <u>scowled</u>. He shook his head <u>sternly</u>.

"You will <u>regret</u> your foolish wish," he said. "I <u>urge</u> you not to be <u>obstinate</u> and <u>persist</u> in this selfish <u>request</u>."

"But you promised!" <u>wailed</u> Midas, beginning to <u>pout</u> like a spoiled child. "Very well, then," said Bacchus, <u>shrugging</u> his shoulders helplessly.

Midas could not wait to test his new power. He hastened out to his garden and embraced a huge tree. Instantly it turned into glistening gold.

"Fabulous! Marvelous!" bellowed Midas gleefully.

Now he scampered around the palace touching chairs and tables. All turned into gold. At last, exhausted and famished, he ordered a feast prepared with all of his favorite food. But when he touched a delicious apple, it, too turned into hard gold. Frantic now, he seized a glass to quench his thirst. The water became a stream of liquid gold. He could no longer eat nor drink!

Suddenly his devoted little daughter came running into the room. She flung herself onto his lap—and when Midas caressed her, promptly became a gold statue.

Midas, now desperate, sought out the wine god and implored him to take back the gift he had so reluctantly bestowed.

"Go then to the river Pactolus and bathe," ordered Bacchus.

Midas hastened to the river and plunged in. When he struck bottom, the river sands became gleaming grains of gold. That is why, say the Greek myths, the sands of the river Pactolus look like gold to this day.

Lesson 53
Vocabulary

1. **encourage** _____ / en kėr′ ij / v.
   antonym: discourage
   The coach <u>encouraged</u> the team before the game.
   The team was <u>discouraged</u> by losing a game.
   nouns: encouragement, discouragement

---

2. **romance** _____ / rō mans′ / n.
   Stories of the old West are called <u>romances</u>.
   Cinderella is about a <u>romance</u> between a prince and a poor girl.
   adjective: romance

---

3. **sculptor** _____ / skulp′ tər / n.
   The work of a <u>sculptor</u> is called sculpture.
   noun: sculpture

---

4. **ivory** _____ / ī′ vər ē / n., adj.
   Piano keys were once made of <u>ivory</u>. (n.)
   Her wedding dress was <u>ivory</u> satin. (adj.)
   noun: ivories

---

5. **temper** _____ / tem′ pər / n., v.
   synonym: disposition (n.)
   My aunt has a sweet <u>temper</u>. (n.)
   The man showed his <u>temper</u> by screaming. (n.)
   <u>Temper</u> your words with kindness. (v.)
   related noun: temperament
   adjective: temperamental

---

6. **sullen** _____ / sul′ ən / adj.
   synonyms: sulky, pouty
   antonym: cheerful
   Tom is <u>sullen</u> because he didn't get his way.

7. **inferior** _____ / in fir′ ē ər / adj.
   synonym: lower
   antonym: higher, superior
   Beth's grades are <u>inferior</u> to yours because she didn't study.
   A private in the army is <u>inferior</u> in rank to a corporal.
   noun: inferiority

8. **studio** _____ / stü′ dē ō / n.
   synonym: workroom
   A painter needs a <u>studio</u> with plenty of light.
   There are many movie <u>studios</u> in Hollywood.

9. **masculine** _____ / mas′ kyə lən / adj.
   synonym: manly, mannish
   antonym: feminine
   <u>Masculine</u> voices are deeper than <u>feminine</u> voices.
   Robert is usually a <u>masculine</u> name.

10. **temple** _____ / tem′ pəl / n.
    A <u>temple</u> is a place of worship.
    homograph: temple (the flattened place on the side of your forehead.)

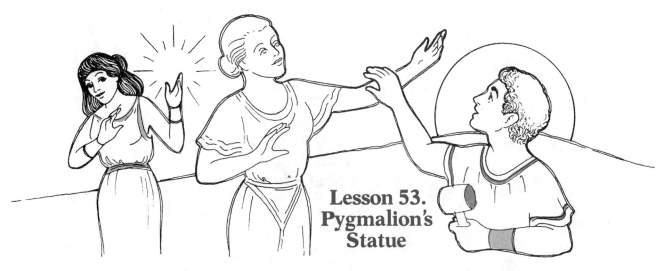

Lesson 53. Pygmalion's Statue

Venus, the Roman goddess of love and beauty, constantly sought to encourage romance among mortals. She was annoyed by an obstinate young man named Pygmalion. He was a haughty sculptor who despised the most attractive and charming maidens of Greece. He did not hesitate to express his feelings publicly.

"These damsels have serious faults. Some are vain and arrogant. Some have violent tempers. Some grow sullen and pout. I will never marry," he declared. "A wife would interfere with the progress of my brilliant artistic career."

In an effort to embarrass Venus, he resolved to create a magnificent ivory statue of a young woman.

"Then all may perceive how inferior our native women really are," he declared.

The statue, which he named Galatea, was gorgeous. Scores of spectators swarmed into Pygmalion's studio to gaze at Galatea by the hour. Presently the rash young sculptor himself began to stare at her until—he fell head over heels in love with her! His masculine prejudices now forgotten, he hastened to Venus' temple. There he implored the goddess to find him a maiden similar to his beloved Galatea. Back at his studio, he again gazed yearningly at his statue and caressed her dainty hands. To his astonishment, the normally cold ivory began to feel warm. Presently she stirred, turned to him, smiled, and gently embraced him!

Pygmalion suddenly realized that Venus had responded to his plea and mysteriously transformed his ivory Galatea into a living mortal. You may be sure Pygmalion, happily wedded to Galatea, never again ridiculed the maidens of his realm.

Lesson 54
Vocabulary

1. **oppose** _____ / ə pōz / v.
   synonym: resist
   Father <u>opposed</u> selling our house.
   John <u>opposed</u> me in a game of checkers.
   Night is <u>opposed</u> to day.
   nouns: opposites, opponent, opposition
   adjective: opposite

---

2. **athlete** _____ / ath′ lēt / n.
   Many <u>athletes</u> take part in the Olympic Games.
   related noun: athletics / ath let′ iks /
   adjective: athletic / ath let′ ik /

---

3. **suitor** _____ / süt′ ər / n.
   The beautiful lady had many <u>suitors</u>.
   The prince was Cinderella's <u>suitor</u>.

---

4. **provide** _____ / prə vīd / v.
   Mother <u>provided</u> cake for the party.
   The barn <u>provided</u> shelter from the rain.
   noun: provisions, provision

---

5. **burst** _____ / bėrst / v.
synonym: explode, break (out)
The balloon <u>burst</u> with a bang.
The house <u>burst</u> into flames.
verb forms: burst, burst, has burst

6. **detain** _____ / də tān′ / v.
synonyms: delay, hold (back)
The rain <u>detained</u> us for an hour.
We were <u>detained</u> after school.
noun: detention

7. **sprint** _____ / sprint / n., v.
synonym: run
Alice <u>sprinted</u> down the street to catch the bus. (v.)
Some athletes take a <u>sprint</u> every day. (n.)
related noun: sprinter

8. **tempt** _____ / tempt / v.
The good food <u>tempted</u> me to eat.
Are you ever <u>tempted</u> to watch TV when you should be studying?
noun: temptation

9. **award** _____ / ə wärd / n., v.
synonyms: prize (n.), grant, give (v.)
Many high schools <u>award</u> scholarships. (v.)
Our dog won an <u>award</u> at the dog show. (n.)

10. **altar** _____ / ôl′ tər / n.
The most beautiful place in our church is the <u>altar</u>.
homonym: alter / ôl′ tər / v. (change)
We <u>altered</u> our plans.

Lesson 54.
Atalanta's Race

Like Pygmalion, the <u>attractive</u> <u>maiden</u> Atalanta was <u>vio</u>-<u>lently</u> <u>opposed</u> to getting married. She was a <u>marvelous</u> <u>ath</u>-<u>lete</u>, and she <u>delighted</u> in <u>constantly</u> outrunning her <u>masculine</u> <u>rivals</u> in foot races.

<u>Scores</u> of <u>gallant</u> young men <u>swarmed</u> about Atalanta's <u>wealthy</u> father's palace, <u>seeking</u> to <u>wed</u> her. At last the <u>annoyed</u> father <u>devised</u> a <u>crafty</u> <u>scheme</u> to <u>reduce</u> the number of Atalanta's <u>suitors</u>. In order to win her hand he <u>proclaimed</u>, the <u>suitor</u> had to beat her in a foot race—or lose his head.

A <u>handsome</u> young prince named Hippomenes, having heard <u>rumors</u> of Atalanta's <u>feminine</u> <u>charms</u>, <u>investigated</u> and <u>resolved</u> to <u>challenge</u> her to a race. He <u>prudently</u> <u>appealed</u> first to Venus, the love goddess, for help. The goddess, always willing to <u>encourage</u> <u>romance</u>, <u>provided</u> him with three <u>gleaming</u> gold apples. Then she slyly whispered her plan for him to win the race—and the <u>reluctant</u> <u>maiden</u>.

An <u>official</u> gave the <u>signal</u> to start the race. Atalanta <u>in</u>-<u>stantly</u> <u>burst</u> into the lead. Before she could <u>achieve</u> too great a lead, though, Hippomenes <u>tossed</u> a golden apple in her path in order to <u>detain</u> her. <u>Momentarily</u> <u>distracted</u>, Atalanta <u>instinc</u>-<u>tively</u> <u>paused</u> to pick up the glistening object. Hippomenes, <u>panting</u> hard, <u>sprinted</u> ahead. Atalanta's <u>superior</u> <u>ability</u> soon enabled her to <u>catch</u> up and pass him.

<u>Desperately</u> Hippomenes <u>tempted</u> her with his second ap-ple. Atalanta could not <u>resist</u> <u>darting</u> aside to <u>secure</u> it, but she promptly <u>resumed</u> her <u>former</u> speed.

As the two <u>approached</u> the finish line, Atalanta was again <u>several</u> steps ahead. Hippomenes cleverly rolled the third ap-ple into the weeds beside the track. Once more Atalanta <u>hesi</u>-<u>tated</u> a <u>moment</u> before she decided to get it. With one last <u>effort</u>, Hippomenes <u>burst</u> <u>triumphantly</u> across the finish line. Of course, he was <u>awarded</u> the Greek <u>symbol</u> of victory, the <u>laurel</u> <u>wreath</u>—and the hand of the blushing Atalanta, who did not at all <u>regret</u> going to the <u>altar</u> with the <u>handsome</u> prince.

Lesson 55
Mastery Test

The Vocabulary Booster lesson for today is your Mastery Test for Lessons 45–54.

☐ Prepare for the Mastery Test by reviewing your notebook pages for Lessons 45–54.

☐ Your teacher will distribute the test. Underline the word or phrase that gives the best definition of the test word. The first one is done for you.

EXAMPLE:

1. **scowl** a) scream b) cover c) <u>frown</u> d) make plans

☐ Review the test with your teacher and class.

☐ Record your Mastery Test score on the Mastery Test Progress Chart at the back of the book.

Lesson 56
Vocabulary

1. **bold** _____ / bōld / adj.
   synonyms: brave, daring, forward
   antonyms: cowardly, bashful
   Hunger makes some animals <u>bold</u>.
   A <u>bold</u> fireman rushed into the burning house to save the child.
   A <u>bold</u> woman pushed ahead of me in line.

   _____

2. **plot** _____ / plot / n., v.
   synonyms: plan, scheme
   Rebels <u>plotted</u> to overthrow the king. (v.)
   The king found out about the rebels' <u>plot</u>. (n.)
   Mother has a garden <u>plot</u>. (n.)
   The story has a good <u>plot</u>. (n.)

   _____

3. **foe** _____ / fō / n.
   synonym: enemy, opponent
   antonym: friend, supporter
   The soldiers fought their <u>foe</u> bravely.
   The mayor is a <u>foe</u> of higher taxes.

   _____

4. **harsh** _____ / härsh / adj.
   synonyms: cruel, stern, hoarse
   The king was a <u>harsh</u> ruler.
   The judge gave the thief a <u>harsh</u> sentence.
   The crow has a <u>harsh</u> cry.
   adverb: harshly

   _____

5. **subject** _____ / sub′ jikt / n., adj.,
   / səb jekt′ / v.
   A tyrant treats his subjects harshly. (n.)
   The subject of my report is "George Washington." (n.)
   I'm subject to head colds in winter. (adj.)
   The pioneers were subjected to many hardships. (v.)

6. **banquet** _____ / bang′ kwit / n.
   synonym: feast
   The senator was the main speaker at the banquet.

7. **assign** _____ / ə sīn′ / v.
   The teacher assigned our arithmetic homework.
   The soldier was assigned to guard duty.
   noun: assignment

8. **view** _____ / vū / n., v.
   The class viewed a film yesterday. (v.)
   My first view of the ocean was exciting. (n.)

9. **inquire** _____ / in kwīr′ / v.
   synonym: ask
   "Where is my hat?" he inquired.
   noun: inquiry / in′ kwə rē̆ /
   adjectives: inquisitive, inquiring

10. **glimpse** _____ / glimps / n., v.
    synonym: glance
    We waited for a glimpse of the singer. (n.)
    I glimpsed a deer as we drove by. (v.)

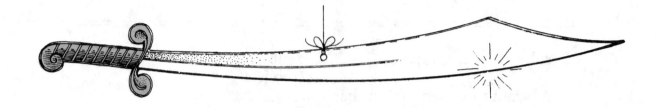

Lesson 56.
The Sword of Damocles

Dionysius, <u>sovereign</u> lord of the city of Syracuse, on the island of Sicily, <u>reigned</u> <u>prudently</u>, but with an iron hand. He was a <u>bold</u> <u>monarch</u>. He made many enemies, who <u>constantly</u> <u>schemed</u> and <u>plotted</u> to <u>betray</u> him and <u>occupy</u> his throne. Because he dealt with his <u>foes</u> so <u>harshly</u>, he became known as the <u>Tyrant</u> of Syracuse.

Dionysius' best friend, Damocles, both admired and <u>envied</u> the <u>Tyrant</u>.

"You are the most <u>fortunate</u> man in the world," he would <u>declare</u>. "You are a <u>wealthy</u> man with an <u>enormous</u> <u>fortune</u>. You have a <u>majestic</u> palace. You have <u>achieved</u> <u>fame</u> for your <u>fabulous</u> <u>military</u> <u>feats</u>. Your <u>loyal</u> subjects praise and <u>flatter</u> you."

Dionysius <u>shrugged</u> his shoulders.

"Would you really <u>prefer</u> to change places with me?" asked Dionysius.

"Why," <u>stammered</u> Damocles, "I never—"

"Why not change places for just one day?" <u>urged</u> his friend.

Damocles was easily <u>persuaded</u> to <u>accept</u> his <u>generous</u> friend's offer. The next day he was <u>provided</u> with <u>royal</u> <u>garments</u>. The <u>officials</u> <u>saluted</u> him <u>courteously</u>. A <u>magnificent</u> <u>banquet</u> was prepared in his honor. Damocles was <u>assigned</u> to a seat in full <u>view</u> of the <u>assembled</u> <u>guests</u>. <u>Spying</u> Dionysius seated <u>opposite</u> him, he raised his wine glass to <u>salute</u> him. As he <u>glanced</u> upward, though, he caught a <u>glimpse</u> of a <u>gleaming</u> sword dangling <u>perilously</u> on a <u>slender</u> thread right over his head. He <u>gasped</u> in <u>terror</u>.

170

"What has startled you?" inquired Dionysius.

"The sword!" whispered Damocles frantically. "Don't you see it?"

"Of course I see it," replied Dionysius calmly. "Such a sword, or one similar to it, hangs daily over the head of every monarch who rules. If you yearn to be a ruler like me, you must live with a fatal sword hanging grimly over your head."

Damocles rose.

"Take back your royal seat," he said humbly. "I will never again covet the wealth and power of a ruler."

Lesson 57
Vocabulary

1. **occur** _____ / ə kėr' / v.
   synonym: happen
   Storms often occur in spring.
   A good idea just occurred to me.
   verb forms: occur, occurred, occurring
   noun: occurrence

---

2. **earnest** _____ / ėr' nist / adj.
   synonyms: serious, thoughtful
   The boss wants earnest workers.
   Mary has an earnest wish to go to college.
   adverb: earnestly

---

3. **construct** _____ / kən strukt' / v.
   synonym: build
   A house is being constructed next door.
   Have you ever constructed a model airplane?
   nouns: constructor, construction
   adjective: constructive

---

4. **flight** _____ / flīt / n.
   synonym: flying
   Our plane flight took two hours.
   verb: fly

---

5. **glide** _____ / glīd / n., v.
   synonym: slide
   Skaters glided across the ice. (v.)
   The plane came down in a smooth glide. (n.)

6. **spray** _____ / sprā / n., v.
   synonym: mist (n.)
   A spray from the hose got the sidewalk wet. (n.)
   The children sprayed each other with the hose. (v.)
   homograph: spray (bunch of flowers)

7. **ray** _____ / rā / n.
   synonyms: beam, gleam
   Rays of sunlight came through the trees.
   We have a ray of hope that our dog will be found.

8. **thrill** _____ / thril / n., v.
   Some people do stunts for a thrill. (n.)
   A good story thrills most children. (v.)
   adjective: thrilling

9. **collapse** _____ / kə laps' / n., v.
   synonyms: crumple, cave in, fall
   The bridge collapsed in the flood. (v.)
   Mr. Hill's business collapsed. (v.)
   Fire caused the collapse of the barn. (n.)

10. **altitude** _____ / al' tə tüd / n.
    synonym: height
    Airplanes fly at altitudes above the clouds.
    In very high altitudes snow doesn't melt.

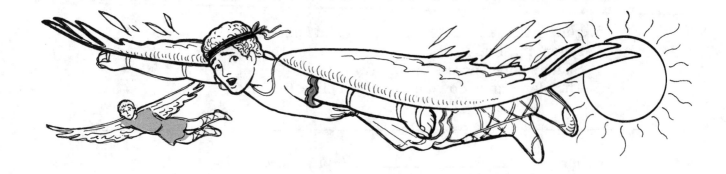

Lesson 57.
The First Flight

Harsh King Minos, the tyrannical monarch of ancient Crete, once held captive a brilliant inventor named Daedalus. Daedalus, a marvelous sculptor, had built him a fabulous garden. He had also erected a magnificent dwelling for the wealthy island sovereign.

Captive Daedalus and his son Icarus obstinately persisted in attempting to devise a scheme to escape the island. Presently a daring plan occurred to the shrewd father. While strolling on the beach, he began in earnest to study the scores of birds that constantly fluttered by or hovered over their heads. He observed daily how they ascended and descended without visible effort.

Crafty Daedalus and his son began to gather the feathers that floated frequently to the ground. To construct two pairs of wings, he glued the feathers to flexible wooden frames that he made from the limbs of trees. Presently he was able to provide wings that could support them in flight.

Flapping their new wings vigorously, the two learned to take off, glide, and land. Clumsy at first, they gradually made progress in learning to sustain themselves in the air.

"We are ready," declared Daedalus at last. "Take heed now to what I saw. Do not swoop too low, for the ocean spray may loosen our wing feathers. Do not be tempted to soar too high. We live in a temperate region, but the sun's rays can become hot at higher altitudes. They may melt the wax I used to hold the feathers together."

At Daedalus' signal, the two balanced themselves and leaped boldly into space. Icarus, thrilled with his new ability to fly, rashly forgot his father's prudent counsel. Higher and higher he ventured. Before he realized what was happening, the sun had melted the exposed wax in his wing feathers. When his wings collapsed, the boy panicked and desperately wailed for help. Mournfully and mutely the elderly father, unable to rescue him, had to watch his son plunge to his death in the sea far below. So ended man's first fatal flight.

Lesson 58
Vocabulary

1. **guardian** _____ / gär′ dē ən / n.
   synonyms: watchman, caretaker
   Pam's uncle became her <u>guardian</u> after her parents died.
   Our watchdog is a faithful <u>guardian</u>.

2. **timber** _____ / tim′ bər / n.
   synonyms: wood, trees
   <u>Timber</u> covers about a third of the United States.

3. **alarm** _____ / ə lärm′ / n., v.
   synonyms: fear (n.), frighten (v.)
   You feel <u>alarm</u> when danger is near. (n.)
   We heard the fire <u>alarm</u> and left the building. (n.)
   Loud noise <u>alarms</u> babies. (v.)
   adjective: alarming

4. **beam** _____ / bēm / n., v.
   synonyms: ray (n.), shine (v.)
   A <u>beam</u> of light came from under the door. (n.)
   The roof is supported by strong <u>beams</u>. (n.)
   The sun <u>beamed</u> brightly. (v.)
   The winning team <u>beamed</u> with pride. (v.)

5. **headlong** _____ / hed′ long′ / adj., adv.
   Matt fell <u>headlong</u> into the dirt. (adv.)
   He took a <u>headlong</u> tumble. (adj.)

6. **treacherous** _____ / trech′ ə rəs / adj.
   synonym: deceitful, dangerous
   A traitor is treacherous.
   Mountain climbing is a treacherous sport.
   noun: treachery

7. **endure** _____ / en dür′ / v.
   synonym: bear
   The sick woman endured a lot of pain.
   "I can't endure this noise!" cried Mother.
   noun: endurance
   adjective: enduring

8. **hearty** _____ / här′ tē / adj.
   synonym: warm, friendly
   Our friends gave us a hearty welcome.
   The campers ate a hearty breakfast.
   adverb: heartily

9. **prospect** _____ / pros′ pekt / n.
   The prospect of a trip made Jane happy.
   Fran has the prospect of a new job.
   noun: prospects
   adjective: prospective

10. **opposite** _____ / op′ ə sit / adj.
    Opposite words are called antonyms.
    Johnny lives at the opposite end of town.
    Dad sat opposite me at lunch.
    verb: oppose

Lesson 58.
Horatius at the Bridge

The enormous enemy army was marching against Rome, and the inferior Roman military force was no match for the invaders. Rome's prospects were indeed gloomy. The huge enemy army would have to cross the Tiber River. That swift stream could be crossed only by means of a single bridge constructed entirely of wood.

The sturdy guardian of that bridge was Horatius. With alarm he saw the superior army assemble on the opposite bank of the river of the Tiber.

"Provide me with two volunteers," said Horatius calmly. "We can hold the bridge for a while. We will attempt to defend the bridge long enough for you to chop it down. Our only hope is to destroy the bridge."

Encouraged by Horatius' prudent counsel, the Romans seized their axes and proceeded in earnest with their perilous assignment. Horatius and his two bold companions grimly hastened to the end of the narrow bridge. The enemy soldiers roared with laughter when they saw only three patriotic defenders there to oppose them.

Again and again three enemy soldiers hurled themselves at the bridge's defenders. Again and again Horatius and his gallant comrades flung their foes back, without faltering. The Romans continued to hack down the huge wooden timbers that supported the bridge. At last their work was done, and the men scrambled back to shore.

"Come back!" bellowed the workers. "The bridge is collapsing."

Horatius' weary companions sprinted safely across the swaying bridge. The great beams suddenly plunged into the river. Only Horatius remained on the opposite bank. He leaped headlong into the treacherous river and swam for shore. The assembled Romans burst into hearty applause. They hoisted him to their shoulders and carried him triumphantly into the city. The statue they erected in his honor stood for several centuries in the Roman marketplace. The thrilling legend of his marvelous feat has endured far longer.

Lesson 59
Vocabulary

1. **territory** _____ / ter′ ə tôr′ ē / n.
   synonyms: land, region, area
   Much <u>territory</u> in North Africa is desert.
   Alaska was once called a <u>Territory</u>.

2. **valley** _____ / val′ ē / n.
   Soil in a river <u>valley</u> is rich.
   Our state has beautiful hills and <u>valleys</u>.

3. **scene** _____ / sēn / n.
   synonyms: view, sight, picture
   The sunset was a lovely <u>scene</u>.
   The artist painted a <u>scene</u> of the forest.
   A crowd gathered at the <u>scene</u> of the accident.
   The <u>scene</u> of the play is New York.
   related noun: scenery
   adjective: scenic
   homonym: seen / sēn / v.
   Have you <u>seen</u> my hat?

4. **blunt** _____ / blunt / v., adj.
   synonym: dull
   antonym: sharp (adj.)
   <u>Blunt</u> knives don't cut well. (adj.)
   <u>Blunt</u> words can hurt a person's feelings. (adj.)
   Cutting metal can <u>blunt</u> a knife. (v.)

5. **slay** _____ / slā / v.
   synonym: kill
   The knight went to <u>slay</u> his foe.
   The brave knight <u>slew</u> the dragon.
   The monster has been <u>slain</u>.
   verb forms: slay, slew, has slain
   homonym: sleigh / slā / n.
   We took a <u>sleigh</u> ride in the snow.

6. **consent** _____ / kən sent' / n., v.
   synonyms: agreement, permission (n.),
   agree (to), permit (v.)
   Dad gave his <u>consent</u> to our plan. (n.)
   Bob <u>consented</u> to sell me his bike. (v.)

7. **brook** _____ / brùk / n.
   synonyms: creek, stream
   The <u>brook</u> has clear, cold water.
   homograph: brook (put up with)
   He <u>brooks</u> no nonsense.

8. **staff** _____ / staf / n.
   synonym: rod, pole, stick
   The flag hung from a <u>staff</u>.
   The boss has a <u>staff</u> of workers.
   The music <u>staff</u> has five lines and four spaces.
   plural noun: staves (rods), staffs (workers)

9. **whirl** _____ / hwėrl / n., v.
   synonym: spin, turn
   The dancers <u>whirled</u> about. (v.)
   The dancers did fancy <u>whirls</u>. (n.)
   related nouns: whirlpool, whirlwind

10. **nimble** _____ / nim' bəl / adj.
    synonyms: light-footed, clever
    Susan is a <u>nimble</u> dancer.
    Ozzie is a <u>nimble</u> shortstop.
    Billy has a <u>nimble</u> mind.

Lesson 59.
David and Goliath

The treacherous Philistines, ancient foes of the Israelites, were again invading Jewish territory. The two armies were camped on opposite sides of a valley. At dawn each morning a huge Philistine warrior named Goliath lumbered out to challenge the Jews to single combat. Heavily armed, he taunted and jeered at King Saul and his Israelites. The prospect of opposing this titanic rival caused the most gallant Jewish patriot to tremble. King Saul was furious. Mutely they had to endure the giant's daily abuse and scorn. Nobody dared respond.

David, a young shepherd, arrived on the scene as Goliath was bellowing his arrogant threats. His father Jesse had sent him to inquire about his three older brothers who were in military service. David was puzzled.

"Why has nobody volunteered to fight him?" he asked his older brother. "Who would be so rash?" growled the brother sullenly. "The giant would toy with any normal mortal."

"Bah!" exclaimed David indignantly. "The God of our fathers will not forsake us! I would not hesitate to face him myself."

David's blunt comments were reported to King Saul. He summoned the lad to his presence.

"Do you really believe that God would perform a miracle and humble that haughty foe?" he asked earnestly.

"Of course!" declared David. "I've slain scores of savage beasts in the wilderness. Let me face this boastful brute, I implore you."

In desperation Saul finally consented. Flinging aside Saul's heavy armor and weapons, David trotted boldly down to a nearby brook. He tossed his shepherd's staff aside and fitted a smooth stone into his slingshot. Goliath stared at the slender lad in astonishment.

"Am I a dog?" he roared. "A child comes to fight me with a shepherd's staff!"

"You come to me with a sword, spear, and a shield. I come in the name of our God," retorted David.

Calmly he whirled his slingshot around his head and let it fly. The fatal stone struck the startled giant squarely on his forehead. He groaned, swayed, and collapsed in full view of both camps. David sprinted nimbly to his side, seized his great sword, and hacked off his head. Triumphantly he held it high to display it to the cheering Israelites.

Lesson 60
Vocabulary

1. **succeed** _____ / sək sēd' / v.
   antonym: fail
   That business has succeeded while many others have failed.
   Carefully made plans usually succeed.
   noun: success
   adjective: successful
   adverb: successfully

---

2. **tribe** _____ / trīb / n.
   synonyms: group, band, clan
   American Indians belong to tribes.
   Tribes of children filled the park.

---

3. **inherit** _____ / in her' it / v.
   Dotty inherited Aunt Laura's ring.
   noun: inheritance

---

4. **throne** _____ / thrōn / n.
   The emperor was on his royal throne.
   The king's throne stands for his power.
   verbs: enthrone, dethrone

---

5. **possess** _____ / pə ses' / v.
   synonyms: own, have
   Athletes possess skill in sports.
   King Midas possessed a lot of gold.
   nouns: possession, possessor
   adjective: possessive

---

6. **justice** _____ / jus′ tis / n.
   synonym: fairness
   Judges see that people receive justice.
   adjectives: just, unjust

7. **personal** _____ / pėr′ sən əl / adj.
   synonym: private
   antonyms: impersonal, public
   A toothbrush is your personal property.
   Give this work your personal attention.
   Personal questions are not polite.

8. **quest** _____ / kwest / n., v
   synonyms: search
   Some men went West in quest of gold. (n.)
   Knights quested for adventure. (v.)

9. **infant** _____ / in′ fənt / n., adj.
   synonym: baby
   An infant can't care for itself. (n.)
   Our project is in its infant stage. (adj.)
   noun: infancy

10. **squirm** _____ / skwėrm / n., v.
    synonyms: twist, wriggle
    Billy squirmed in his chair. (v.)
    Millie gave a squirm and hung her head in embarrassment. (n.)

Lesson 60.
The Wisdom of Solomon

David <u>succeeded</u> King Saul as <u>sovereign</u> of the twelve <u>tribes</u> of Israel. When he died, his son Solomon <u>inherited</u> the <u>throne</u>. Solomon was <u>modest</u> and <u>humble</u> and afraid that he did not <u>possess</u> the <u>talent</u> to <u>reign</u> <u>prudently</u> over his people.

One night he dreamed that Yahweh, the God of the Jewish people, appeared to him. Yahweh offered to <u>grant</u> him whatever he most desired.

"My <u>subjects</u> <u>frequently</u> <u>appeal</u> to me to <u>provide</u> <u>justice</u> in their <u>disputes</u>," said Solomon. "Please <u>bestow</u> wisdom upon me so I may judge fairly and they may <u>rely</u> upon me."

"Because you have not asked for <u>wealth</u>, I shall make you a <u>fabulously</u> <u>wealthy</u> <u>monarch</u> also," said Yahweh. "You shall <u>erect</u> a <u>magnificent</u> <u>temple</u> that shall bring you great <u>fame</u>."

Solomon <u>displayed</u> <u>shrewd</u> and <u>considerate</u> judgment in <u>resolving</u> his <u>subjects'</u> <u>personal</u> <u>quarrels</u>. Once two women appeared before his <u>throne</u> in <u>quest</u> of justice. One <u>clutched</u> a crying child. The other woman spoke first.

"We gave birth to male <u>infants</u> at about the same time," she said <u>earnestly</u>. "This woman's son <u>perished</u>. During the night she stole my son. She <u>abandoned</u> her dead child in my crib. We live in the same house."

"She lies!" cried the other mother. "The living child is mine! The dead one is hers!"

"Fetch me a sharp sword," Solomon bade his servant. "Now hand me the living child," he continued calmly.

Balancing the squirming infant in one hand, he raised the gleaming weapon and whirled it high over his head.

"I shall cut the living child in half," he declared harshly, "I shall award each of you half. Isn't that fair?"

"Fair enough!" sullenly snarled the one who had been embracing and caressing the infant. She glared triumphantly at the other woman.

"No," protested the other one in a quivering voice. "Do not slay the child I would prefer to yield my claim and have the child live."

"Take the child," said Solomon sympathetically. "It is quite clear that you are the true mother."

Lesson 61
Vocabulary

1. **sultan** _____ / sul′ tən / n.
   synonyms: ruler, sovereign, monarch
   The sultan of Turkey was the most powerful of all.

2. **vizier** _____ / vi zir′ / n.
   The vizier was the sultan's highest official.

3. **horror** _____ / hôr′ ər / n.
   synonyms: terror, fright, fear
   Amy has a horror of snakes.
   verb: horrify
   adjectives: horrible, horrid

4. **confide** _____ / kən fīd′ / v.
   Dottie confides her secrets to her best friend.
   noun: confidence
   adjective: confidential
   adverb: confidentially

5. **instruct** _____ / in strukt′ / v.
   synonyms: teach, direct, order
   Miss Green instructs us in music.
   The owner instructed the agent to sell the house.
   We were instructed to leave the room.
   nouns: instruction, instructor
   adjective: instructive

6. **fascinate** / fas′ ən āt′ / v.
   synonyms: charm, please, delight
   Almost everyone is <u>fascinated</u> by a kitten.
   Which animal at the zoo <u>fascinates</u> you most?
   noun: fascination
   adjective: fascinating

7. **tale** _____ / tāl / n.
   synonym: story
   Fables are <u>tales</u> with morals, or lessons.
   Grandpa told <u>tales</u> of his childhood.
   A person who carries <u>tales</u> is a gossip.
   homonym: tail (A mouse has a long <u>tail</u>.)

8. **adventure** _____ / ad ven′ chər / n.
   The travelers had an <u>adventure</u> in the jungle.
   noun: adventurer
   adjective: adventurous

9. **familiar** _____ / fə mil′ yər / adj.
   synonym: well known
   antonym: unfamiliar
   "Yankee Doodle" is a <u>familiar</u> song.
   I'm not <u>familiar</u> with this road.
   noun: familiarity

10. **decree** _____ / di krē′ / n., v.
    synonyms: law, order (n.), command (v.)
    The tyrant <u>decreed</u> that all rebels be punished. (v.)

Lesson 61.
The Thousand and One Nights

The <u>Arabian Nights</u>, also known as <u>The</u> <u>Thousand</u> <u>and</u> <u>One</u> <u>Nights</u>, is a famous collection of about 100 stories. The <u>Sultan</u> Shahriyar once discovered, to his <u>horror</u>, that his wife had been <u>plotting</u> <u>treacherously</u> with his foes to <u>betray</u> <u>him</u>. The <u>sultan</u>, in a fit of <u>violent</u> <u>temper</u>, <u>impulsively</u> ordered her head chopped off. After <u>brooding</u> <u>sullenly</u> over the <u>betrayal</u>, he became <u>persuaded</u> that no <u>mortal</u> woman could be trusted any longer. He <u>harshly</u> <u>decreed</u> that each girl he brought before the <u>altar</u> should be killed the morning after her wedding. The <u>sultan</u>, who had been a <u>temperate</u> and <u>prudent</u> <u>sovereign</u>, now became <u>heartily</u> <u>despised</u> as a <u>rash</u> and <u>brutal</u> <u>tyrant</u>. His once <u>loyal</u> <u>subjects</u> lived in <u>constant</u> <u>terror</u>, fearing that one of their daughters would be chosen as the <u>sultan's</u> bride.

One day Sheherazade, the <u>gorgeous</u> daughter of the <u>sultan's</u> head <u>official</u>, the grand <u>vizier</u>, <u>volunteered</u> to become the sultan's bride. The <u>alarmed</u> <u>vizier</u>, who was <u>devoted</u> to his clever daughter, <u>objected</u> <u>vigorously</u>. Only when Sheherazade <u>confided</u> that she had an <u>effective</u> plan to stop the <u>sultan's</u> senseless killing did he <u>grant</u> his <u>reluctant</u> <u>consent</u>.

Sheherazade then <u>instructed</u> her sister to make an <u>earnest</u> <u>personal</u> <u>appeal</u> to the <u>sultan</u>.

"My sister has for years told me one of her <u>fabulous</u> stories <u>daily</u>," she said <u>mournfully</u>. "I <u>urge</u> your royal highness to permit her to tell one more tomorrow, on your <u>wedding</u> day. I shall never see her again, you know."

The <u>sultan</u> <u>considerately</u> agreed. Sheherazade <u>craftily</u> stopped her story at its most <u>thrilling</u> point. The <u>sultan</u> was so <u>fascinated</u> by the story that he let her live another day in order to finish the story. The clever girl finished her story, started another, and again stopped at the most interesting point. Sheherazade continued her exciting <u>tales</u> for a thousand and one nights. By that time the <u>sultan</u> was so much in love with his <u>charming</u> wife that he had his law changed. Among the heroes in Sheherazade's <u>Arabian</u> <u>Nights</u> are Aladdin, Ali Baba, and Sinbad. Their <u>adventures</u> have become <u>familiar</u> to readers all over the world.

Lesson 62
Vocabulary

1. **magician** _____ / mə jish′ ən / n.
   <u>Magicians</u> do tricks that seem impossible.
   related noun: magic
   adjective: magical

---

2. **precious** _____ / presh′ əs / adj.
   synonym: valuable
   antonym: worthless
   Diamonds are <u>precious</u> stones.
   Friends are <u>precious</u> to people.

---

3. **blaze** _____ / blāz / n., v.
   synonyms: flame, fire, outburst (n.), burn, shine (v.)
   The campfire made a big <u>blaze</u>. (n.)
   It was hot in the <u>blaze</u> of the sun. (n.)
   The angry man had a <u>blaze</u> of temper. (n.)
   A fire is <u>blazing</u> in the fireplace. (v.)
   The Christmas tree <u>blazed</u> with lights. (v.)

---

4. **mumble** _____ / mum′ bəl / n., v.
   synonym: mutter
   Shy people often <u>mumble</u> instead of speaking clearly. (v.)
   It's hard to understand a <u>mumble</u>. (n.)

---

5. **phrase** _____ / frāz / n.

A phrase is a group of words.

"So long" is a phrase that means goodbye.

6. **chamber** _____ / chām' bər / n.

synonym: room

The palace had many chambers.

The Senate is one chamber of Congress.

Your heart has four chambers or enclosed places.

7. **positive** _____ / poz' ə tiv / adj.

synonyms: sure, certain

I'm positive that I mailed the letter.

adverb: positively

8. **release** _____ / ri lēs' / n., v.

synonym: free (v.)

The prisoner was released from jail. (v.)

Kathy opened the cage and released the bird. (v.)

Jim will be released from the hospital when he is well. (v.)

Good news brings release from worry. (n.)

9. **palm** _____ / päm / n.

I held the chick in the palm of my hand.

homograph: palm (tree)

10. **genie** _____ / jē' nē / n.

synonym: spirit

A genie is a make-believe creature.

Genies were said to do magic for a master.

Lesson 62.
Aladdin's Wonderful Lamp, Part 1

Aladdin and his widowed mother were poor, and the lazy boy did little to help support her. It happened that a treacherous magician came to their city in search of somebody he could use to secure a precious magic lamp. Spying Aladdin strolling by in the swarming streets, he resolved to use him in his sly scheme. Pretending he was the lad's long-lost uncle, he replaced Aladdin's shabby garments and provided the grateful mother with money.

Having gained their confidence, he took Aladdin out into the wilderness. There he built a blazing fire, tossed in a few grains of fragrant powder, and mumbled some magic phrases. The earth quivered and cracked open, revealing a huge stone with a brass ring. The magician instructed Aladdin to lift the stone, squirm through the opening, and descend the stairs.

"You will find a fabulous garden with marvelous fruit trees," he said. "You will also see a brass lamp in plain view. Bring it to me."

The magician removed a curious old ring from his finger and slipped the band on Aladdin's finger. Aladdin hoisted the stone and cautiously ventured into the chambers below. Presently he discovered that the trees sprouted magnificent jewels that glistened and sparkled brilliantly in the dim light. Thrilled at the prospect of becoming wealthy instantly, he hastily stuffed some into his pockets. He found the lamp on an altar. He seized it and scrambled nimbly back to the cave opening.

"Hand me the lamp," growled the magician greedily, thrusting out his hand. Aladdin became suspicious and obstinately refused to give up the lamp until he had emerged from the gloomy cave. The annoyed magician lost his temper, whirled, and flung magic powder on the fire. He furiously muttered the magic phrases again. Instantly the stone rolled to its former place, leaving Aladdin abandoned in the cave.

Aladdin now perceived that the crafty magician had succeeded in deceiving him. He was no uncle. He had simply come in quest of the lamp. Evidently he was not allowed to get it personally.

Forlorn and forsaken, Aladdin sat and wept, positive that he would never be released or rescued. Rubbing his palms in despair, he happened to rub the mysterious ring that he still possessed. Suddenly a hideous genie appeared.

"I am the genie of the ring," he announced. "I am ready to serve you. What are your wishes?"

Lesson 63
Vocabulary

1. **relate** _____ / ri lāt′ / v.
   synonyms: tell, connect
   Uncle Jack related tales of his childhood.
   You are related to the members of your family.
   Health and happiness are related.
   nouns: relationship, relatives

---

2. **mist** _____ / mist / n., v.
   synonyms: haze, fog (n.)
   There is a mist over the pond in the morning. (n.)
   It's misting outside today. (v.)
   adjective: misty

---

3. **obedient** _____ / ō be′ dē ənt / adj.
   antonym: disobedient
   Our old dog is obedient, but the new puppy is disobedient.
   noun: obedience
   verb: obey

---

4. **eager** _____ / ē′ gər / adj.
   We were eager for the play to start.
   She is an eager student who wants to learn a lot.
   noun: eagerness
   adverb: eagerly

---

5. **prolong** _____ / prə long' / v.
   synonyms: lengthen, extend, stretch
   antonym: shorten
   Good health habits can prolong life.
   Betty prolonged the story by adding details.

6. **launch** _____ / lônch / n., v.
   synonyms: start, begin (v.)
   Our country will soon launch another spaceship. (v.)
   The senator launched his campaign for reelection. (v.)
   The man launched into a long speech. (v.)

7. **account** _____ / ə kount' / n.
   synonyms: story, report, record
   Joan gave an account of her trip.
   Do you have a bank account?
   The phrase on account of means because of.

8. **avenge** _____ / ə venj' / v.
   The angry man vowed to avenge his brother's death.
   noun: revenge, vengeance

9. **court** _____ / kôrt / n., v.
   There is a court between the buildings. (n.)
   We play tennis on a tennis court. (n.)
   A judge hears evidence in court. (n.)
   The king and his court went to the ball. (n.)
   The prince courted Cinderella. (v.)

10. **recover** _____ / ri kuv' ər / v.
    The police recovered the stolen car.
    The girl recovered from her illness.
    noun: recovery

Lesson 63.
Aladdin's Wonderful Lamp, Part 2

"Get me out of here!" gasped Aladdin frantically to the ring genie that had mysteriously appeared. Instantly the astonished lad found himself outside the cave chambers. He hastily trudged home and related all that had occurred. Mother and son were famished, so Aladdin, forgetting the miraculous services he could secure from the ring genie, proposed to sell the brass lamp he had found on the altar. As the lamp was soiled, the mother began to rub it clean. Instantly another enormous, hideous genie appeared in a cloud of dense mist.

"I am the genie of the lamp," he proclaimed in a deep bass voice. "I am ready to serve you. What are your wishes?"

"We're hungry. Bring us something to eat," exclaimed Aladdin.

The genie disappeared, but promptly returned bearing delicious fare piled on gleaming plates of precious silver.

Aladdin and his mother prospered and became fabulously wealthy as a result of the obedient service of the genies of the ring and the lamp. Sheherazade related to the fascinated sultan a long series of exciting tales about Aladdin's further adventures. Of course, she broke off each story at the most thrilling point. The sultan eagerly persisted in prolonging her life in order to hear the outcome.

Sheherazade launched into a romantic account of how Aladdin courted and married the sultan's handsome daughter. The treacherous magician later returned with his brother to avenge himself on Aladdin and make Aladdin's wife a captive. Aladdin cleverly got her released and recovered her from the villain's clutches. Several years later he succeeded to the sultan's throne. He reigned prudently and justly as sovereign over the subjects of his native realm.

Lesson 64
Vocabulary

1. **interrupt** _____ / in′ tə rupt′ / v.
   Don't interrupt the speaker.
   A phone call interrupted our dinner.
   noun: interruption

_____

2. **abrupt** _____ / ə brupt′ / adj.
   synonyms: sudden, unexpected
   Paul made an abrupt stop on his bike when a dog ran in front of him.
   The music came to an abrupt end.
   adverb: abruptly

_____

3. **Sesame** _____ / ses′ ə mē / n.
   "Open Sesame" was a storybook password.
   related noun: sesame seeds

_____

4. **gallop** _____ / gal′ əp / n., v.
   synonym: run
   A horse runs fastest when it gallops. (v.)
   I galloped home after school. (v.)
   Off the horse went at a gallop. (n.)

_____

5. **spacious** ———————————— / spā′ shəs / adj.
   synonyms: large, roomy
   The school has a spacious playground.
   noun: space

6. **cavern** ———————————— / kav′ ərn / n.
   synonym: cave
   Mammoth Cave is a cavern in Kentucky.

7. **manage** ———————————— / man′ ij / v.
   The principal manages school affairs.
   Did you manage to get the car started?
   The poor widow managed on very little money.
   nouns: manager, management

8. **sufficient** ———————————— / sə fish′ ənt / adj.
   synonym: enough
   antonym: insufficient
   I've had sufficient time to get ready.
   The campers had insufficient water for their long hike.
   adverb: sufficiently

9. **detail** ———————————— / dē′ tāl / n., v.
   synonym: (small) part (n.)
   Alice told every detail of her trip. (n.)
   She detailed everything she did. (v.)

10. **climax** ———————————— / klī′ maks / n., v.
    synonym: peak (n.)
    The climax of the story is the most exciting part. (n.)
    Seeing the Grand Canyon was the climax of our trip. (n.)
    That visit climaxed the whole trip. (v.)

Lesson 64.
Ali Baba and the Forty Thieves, Part 1

Sheherazade obediently launched into another series of fascinating tales, these about Ali Baba. Again she interrupted each story at a thrilling point or climax to encourage the sultan to prolong her life another day.

Once upon a time, she began, there lived two brothers, humble Ali Baba and haughty Cassim. One day Ali Baba was returning home from his daily chores in a forest. Suddenly he heard a band of horsemen approaching. Abandoning his donkey, he clambered nimbly into the dense limbs of a tree. Presently the riders swarmed into view. They dismounted before a huge rock. In a harsh bass voice their leader abruptly cried "Open Sesame!" As he uttered the odd phrase, the rock opened, and the forty riders scrambled inside. Ali Baba was positive that they were a band of thieves that frequently roamed in the region.

Presently they emerged. The leader cried "Shut Sesame!" The rock closed, and the troop of forty thieves galloped off in a cloud of whirling dust.

Ali Baba descended, trotted eagerly to the rock, and hesitantly mumbled, "Open Sesame!" The rock opened. Ali cautiously stepped into the gloomy interior of a spacious cavern. To his astonishment he saw enormous boxes of sparkling gold and silver coins, precious jewels, and similar treasures. He boldly piled all he could manage on his sturdy donkey.

Ali _hastened_ home, _bursting_ to give his wife an _account_ of his _adventure_ and their good fortune. The _delighted_ couple decided to measure their _wealth_. As they _possessed_ no measuring cup, Ali borrowed one from Cassim. Puzzled about his poor brother's need for such a cup, Cassim slyly smeared some _liquid_ paste in it.

When the cup returned, _suspicious_ Cassim found a _gleaming_ gold coin stuck to the bottom.

"Where did you get _sufficient_ gold to measure?" he _inquired_ _curiously_.

Ali _confided_ in _detail_ a _report_ of his _adventure_ at the cavern. Of course Cassim could not _resist_ the _temptation_ to visit the _mysterious_ _cavern_.

Lesson 65
Vocabulary

1. **thievery** _____ / thēv′ ə rē / n.
   synonym: theft
   Police report less thievery this year.
   noun: thief
   verb: thieve / thēv /
   adjective: thievish

---

2. **corpse** _____ / kôrps / n.
   The corpse of the dead king was dressed in royal robes.
   The Egyptian mummies are ancient corpses.

---

3. **chieftain** _____ / chēf′ tən / n.
   synonyms: chief, leader
   African tribes were led by chieftains.

---

4. **residence** _____ / rez′ ə dəns / n.
   synonyms: house, home
   The White House is the residence of the President.
   related noun: residency
   verb: reside
   adjective: residential

---

5. **rally** _____ / ral′ ē / n., v.
   The class rallied to clean up the schoolyard. (v.)
   The sick girl rallied and got well. (v.)
   We had a rally before the football game. (n.)

6. **foil** _____ / foil / v.
   synonym: outwit
   The police foiled the robbers and kept them from stealing the money.
   homographs: foil (tin paper)
                  foil (long thin sword)

7. **locate** _____ / lō′ kāt / v.
   Can you locate Missouri on the map?
   St. Louis is located on the Mississippi River.
   noun: location

8. **crouch** _____ / krouch / n., v.
   synonym: stoop
   The cat crouched near the bird cage. (v.)
   A catcher in a ball game is usually in a crouch. (n.)

9. **mansion** _____ / man′ shən / n.
   The rich family lives in a mansion with many rooms.

10. **additional** _____ / ə dish′ ə nəl / adj.
    synonyms: more, extra
    I need additional help with my work.
    Do you want additional homework?
    noun: addition
    verb: add

Lesson 65.
Ali Baba and the Forty Thieves, Part 2

Greedy Cassim had no trouble getting into the thieves' cavern. Once in the spacious interior, he eagerly stuffed a huge sack with sparkling coins and precious jewels. In his excitement, he forgot the "Sesame" password to get out. Interrupted in his thievery by the brutal robbers, he was instantly slain.

Ali Baba went to investigate. He found Cassim's corpse and mournfully carried it home. Ali, Cassim's widow, and Morgiana, her devoted servant, now devised a crafty scheme to make Cassim's death appear to be from natural causes. Morgiana, however, carelessly paid for Cassim's burial with gold coins from the thieves' cavern.

That mistake enabled the thieves' chieftain to identify Cassim's majestic residence as the place where Ali was hiding. He marked the mansion with an X symbol and galloped back to rally his comrades for a fatal attack on the house. Alert Morgiana, however, foiled the crafty villain by marking all the houses similarly.

The obstinate leader persisted, though, and managed to locate the house again. Plotting to slay Ali, he hastened back with a string of forty sturdy donkeys. Each beast bore two huge olive jars. One was filled with oil. In the other crouched one of the thieves. Morgiana peered into the jars and revealed the plot. She calmly instructed her obedient servants to boil the oil—and to pour the boiling liquid into the jars concealing the thieves!

Sheherazade continued the series of Ali Baba adventures for several additional days. She again paused abruptly at a thrilling point in the account. The sultan, fascinated by the clever plots, continued to prolong the charming storyteller's life another day. Finally, as the thousand and one nights drew to a close, he decreed that no more wives would be slain, and that Sheherazade would reign with him as long as they lived.

Lesson 66
Mastery Test

The Vocabulary Booster lesson for today is your Mastery Test for Lessons 56–65.

☐ Prepare for the Mastery Test by reviewing your notebook pages for Lessons 56–65.

☐ Your teacher will distribute the test. Underline the word or phrase that gives the best definition of the test word. The first one is done for you.

EXAMPLE:

1. **headlong** a) <u>head first</u> b) under c) on top d) not short

☐ Review the test with your teacher and class.

☐ Record your Mastery Test score on the Mastery Test Progress Chart at the back of the book.

Pronunciation Guide
to Proper Names

Lesson 28
Hera   /hir' ə/
Zeus   /züs/
Echo   /ek' ō/
Narcissus   /när sis'əs/

Lesson 29
Callisto   /kə lis' tō/
Arcas   /är' kəs/
Ursa Major   /ėr sə   mā' jər /

Lesson 30
Ceres   /sir' ēz/
Demeter   /di mē tər/
Proserpine   /prō sėr' pə ne/
Persephone   /pər sef' ə nē/
Pluto   /plü' tō/

Lesson 31
Apollo   /ə pol' ō/
Eros   /er' os/
Cupid   /kū' pid/
Aphrodite   /af' rə dī' tē/
Daphne   /daf' nē/

Lesson 32
Coronis   /kə ro' nis/

Lesson 34
Clytie   /klī' tə ē

Lesson 35
Clymene   /klim' ə nē/
Phaethon   /fā' ə thon/
Styx   /stiks/
Hades   /hā' dēz/

Lesson 36
Aurora   /ə rô' rə/
Tithonus   /ti thō' nəs/

Lesson 37
Io   /ī' o/
Argus   /är' gəs/
Hermes   /hėr' mēz/

Lesson 38
Athena   /ə thē' nə/
Arachne   /ə rak' nē/

Lesson 39
Mars   /märz/
Vulcan   /vul' kən/
Ares   /ãr' ēz/
Venus   /vē' nəs/
Alectryon   /ə lek' trē on/

Lesson 40
Pandora   /pan dô' rə/
Epimetheus   /epi mē' thē əs/
Titan   /tīt' ən/

Lesson 41
Cinderella   /sin də rel' ə/

Lesson 45
Bremen   /bre' mən/

Lesson 50
Hamelin   /ham' lən/

Lesson 51
Austria   /ô' strē ə
Gessler   /ges lər/

Lesson 52
Midas   /mī' dəs/
Bacchus   /bak' əs/

Lesson 53
Pygmalion   /pig māl' yen/
Galatea   /gal' ə tē' ə/

Lesson 54
Atalanta   /at'ə lan' tə/
Hippomenes   /hi pom' ə nēz/

Lesson 56
Damocles   /dam' ə klēz/
Dionysius   /di ə nē' sē əs/
Syracuse   /sir' ə kyüs/
Sicily   /sis' ə lē/

Lesson 57
Minos   /mī' nəs/
Daedalus   /ded'əl əs/
Icarus   /ik' ə rəs/

Lesson 58
Horatius   /hə rā' shəs/'
Tiber   /ti' bər/

Lesson 59
Philistine   /fil' əs tēn/
Israelite   /iz' rē əl īt/
Goliath   /gə lī' əth/
Saul   /sôl/

Lesson 60
Solomon   /sol' ə mən/

Lesson 61
Shahriyar   /shä' ri yär/
Sheherazade   /shə he' rə zäd/
Aladdin   /ə lad' ən/
Ali Baba   /al' ē bäb ə/
Sinbad   /sin' bad/

Lesson 64
Cassim   /kə sēm'/

Lesson 65
Ali   /al' ē/
Morgiana   /môr' jē an' ə

Lesson Test
Progress Chart

Use this chart to record your progress throughout the year. Put a dot on the chart to indicate the number of answers you got right on each Lesson Test. Draw a line from dot to dot to indicate your progress.

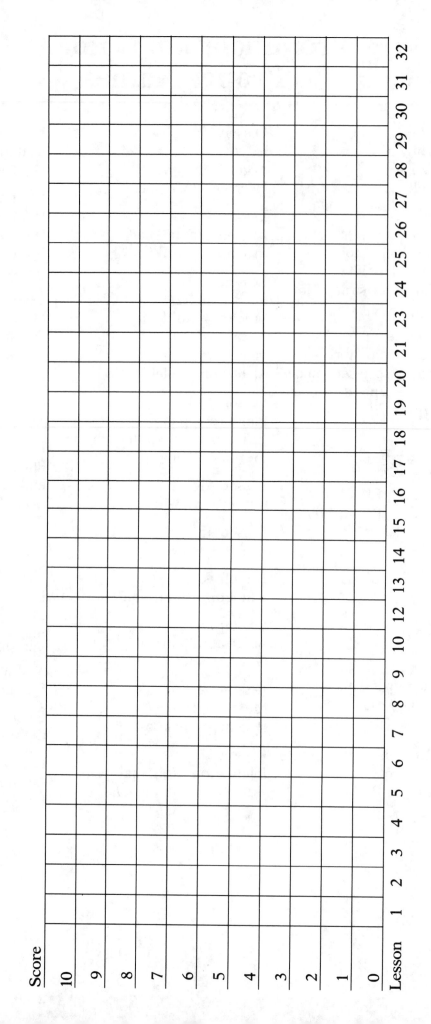

Score																															
10																															
9																															
8																															
7																															
6																															
5																															
4																															
3																															
2																															
1																															
0																															
Lesson	1	2	3	4	5	6	7	8	9	10	11	12	13	14	15	16	17	18	19	20	21	22	23	24	25	26	27	28	29	30	31	32

Lesson Test
Progress Chart

Use this chart to record your progress throughout the year. Put a dot on the chart to indicate the number of answers you got right on each Lesson Test. Draw a line from dot to dot to indicate your progress.

Score

	34	35	36	37	38	39	40	41	42	43	44	45	46	47	48	49	50	51	52	53	54	55	56	57	58	59	60	61	62	63	64	65
10																																
9																																
8																																
7																																
6																																
5																																
4																																
3																																
2																																
1																																
0																																

Lesson

Mastery Test Progress Chart

Use this chart to record your Mastery Test scores throughout the year. Put a dot on the chart to indicate the number of answers you got right on each Mastery Test. Draw a line from dot to dot to indicate your progress. The line will go up as your scores improve. Try to keep your progress line as high as possible.

Score

95						
90						
85						
80						
75						
70						
65						
60						
55						
50						
45						
40						
35						
30						
25						
20						
15						
10						
5						
0						
Test	11	22	33	44	55	66